About the Author

Born in Sheffield in 1950, Bill is now retired and lives with Sheila, his wife of over fifty years. He has enjoyed a diverse life at school, in the army, in employment and in retirement. He is a published music composer and arranger and is also a published author.

Bill continues to contend with the surprises his now grown-up meddlesome rogue gene conjures up to interfere with his life's affairs.

My Grown-Up Rogue Gene

William A. Pollard

My Grown-Up Rogue Gene

Olympia Publishers
London

www.olympiapublishers.com
OLYMPIA PAPERBACK EDITION

Copyright © William A. Pollard 2023

The right of William A. Pollard to be identified as author of
this work has been asserted in accordance with sections 77 and 78 of the
Copyright, Designs and Patents Act 1988.

All Rights Reserved

No reproduction, copy or transmission of this publication
may be made without written permission.
No paragraph of this publication may be reproduced,
copied or transmitted save with the written permission of the publisher,
or in accordance with the provisions of the Copyright Act 1956
(as amended).

Any person who commits any unauthorised act in relation to
this publication may be liable to criminal
prosecution and civil claims for damage.

A CIP catalogue record for this title is
available from the British Library.

ISBN: 978-1-80439-313-0

This is a work of creative nonfiction.
The events are portrayed to the best of the author's memory. While stories
in this book are true, names and identifying details have been omitted to
protect the identity of the people involved.

First Published in 2023

Olympia Publishers
Tallis House
2 Tallis Street
London
EC4Y 0AB

Printed in Great Britain

Dedication

To Sophie, Adam, Kelley, Hayley, Ashar... And Kimberley who likes to be called Kim. My grandchildren... What a bunch of characters they are! Every one cherished by Sheila and myself for the joy they bring to us. May they all grow up without too much interference from their rogue gene.

Acknowledgements

My thanks to Joe Edwards (Automotive Engineering Ltd., Leighton Buzzard) and John Creasey who gave me permission to photo the Land Rover images in chapter 4, to John Cook who helped me to improve my images, to Victoria Wise (Friends of Birley Spa) who gave me permission to use the photo of The Bath House in chapter 11 and to Frank Suess for his photo of the skiff in chapter 22.

Thanks, also, to my wife Sheila who has audited every word of every chapter in both my books. Her words of wisdom helped me make sense of my musings.

Finally, I'd like to thank all those un-named people mentioned in my autobiographies. Without them I wouldn't have had any material to write about.

CONTENTS

Bill's Prologue 15

BOOK 1 - COMMUNICATION
Chapter 1
   Bill's Sheffield Lingo 21
Chapter 2
   Bill's Cautious Answer 25
Chapter 3
   Bill's Precarious Encounter 27
Chapter 4
   Bill's Convoy 30
Chapter 5
   Bill's Wedding 39
Chapter 6
   Bill Farting 45
Chapter 7
   Bill's Insurance Howlers 48

BOOK 2 - EMPLOYMENT
Chapter 8
   Bill Signing On 53
Chapter 9
   Bill's First Ever Job Interview 61
Chapter 10
   Bill's First Mortgage 66
Chapter 11
   Bill's Bath House 71
Chapter 12
   Bill's Cracks 75
Chapter 13
   Bill Moves On 81
Chapter 14
   Bill's Adjustments 86
Chapter 15
   Bill's Tempest 91

Chapter 16
    Bill's Close Calls In A Smart Suit 95
Chapter 17
    Bill's Many Frustrations 101
Chapter 18
    Bill's Advanced Education 110
Chapter 19
    Bill's Return To The Treadmill 113
Chapter 20
    Bill's Farewell To The Treadmill 118

BOOK 3 - HOLIDAYS

Chapter 21
    Bill Under Canvas 126
Chapter 22
    Bill Messing About On The River 131
Chapter 23
    Bill's Introduction To Motor Cruising 138
Chapter 24
    Bill's Cruise On The Norfolk Broads 146
Chapter 25
    Bill's Family Cruise On The Thames 153
Chapter 26
    Bill's Big Boats 160
Chapter 27
    Bill's Brush With The Law 167
Chapter 28
    Bill's Surprise Cruise 173
Chapter 29
    Bill's Colorado Experience 179
Chapter 30
    Bill's Jest 181
Chapter 31
    Bill's Close Call In A Lock 187
Chapter 32
    Bill's Fishing Trip 190

BOOK 4 - THAT'S LIFE

Chapter 33
    Grumpy Old Bill 200
Chapter 34
    Bill's Technology 209
Chapter 35
    Bill's Health 217
Chapter 36
    Bill's Coincidences 231

Bill's Epilogue 237

BILL'S PROLOGUE

You may already know this from my previous book but I'll remind you anyway. I've got a rogue gene.

You know what? With the exception of the Pollard clan everybody else in the world must lead pretty boring lives. Nothing ever happens to them. They go about their business and get to the end of the day without encountering a single hiccup in their lifestyle. Not so with the Pollards! Absolutely everything we do is influenced by a rogue gene that sometimes makes life for us really complicated.

Take shopping, for instance. Just about every time I go for my weekly shop at our local supermarket, I trigger the alarms on my way out. It doesn't matter how much I've spent or what bag checks I've been subjected to I always set off the door alarm on my way out. The staff have got to know me by now and they just wave me through. Everybody else gets out with a free pass without any beep, beep, beeps... Not me!

Airports are a constant source of body searches and pat-downs because I cannot go through the security arch without it shouting for a guard to come and scan me, as if I had hidden my barcode of life somewhere private.

Even restaurants have started beeping 'Not paid! Not paid! Not paid!,' even though my credit card has just taken a massive hit for a meal for my wife and me.

Yet everybody else seems to leave the building... Any building, without any intrusive and embarrassing beeping. What is it about them that gives them a free pass and not me?

I've still got the same rogue gene that featured in my previous book! The bloody little troublemaker has never given me any decent support from the time I departed from the army. Frustratingly, it has continued to grow with me and it is now a grown-up rogue gene. A skilled and proficient grown-up rogue gene!

Galling, eh? Really annoying.

You'll gather that this malevolent, repugnant, unpopular creature has transformed me into something worse than a grumpy old man. As a result of its influence over the years, I have morphed from being a grumpy old man to being a grumpier old man, but I don't suppose I'm alone on that level, am I? Hands up those of you who have got a subscription to that particular club...

I still haven't given my grown-up rogue gene a proper name. I've called it all sorts of uncomplimentary and unmentionable names each and every time it has interfered with my life's itinerary, but I don't consider it worthy of a permanent name. If I do that it's possible that I'll feel some empathy towards it. I just call it 'Grown-up rogue gene.'

Over the years this evil object has done everything possible to complicate my life. From causing mayhem and a great many everyday problems to even engineering my departure from the army. It is permanently in the background, waiting for the opportunity to destroy my hopes, aspirations, dreams and strategies. It's true.

Some would call this bad luck but it's not. It is interference of the highest order. Life changing, head banging, trouble-making interference.

Anyway, grown-up rogue gene continues to hide in the folds of my ballbag, loafing around and just waiting to pounce. I can't do anything about it because I was born with it, inherited from some distant relative that somehow produced a mutated gene gone rogue and anti-social.

I was born in Sheffield, Yorkshire, in May 1950. I'm sure I've asked this before but did you know that Yorkshire is the centre of the Universe? No? Well, it is. For those of you, like me, who are rubbish at sums that birth date makes me seventy-two years old at the time of writing (2022).

I got to this age without any support whatsoever from my grown-up rogue gene and I've suffered uncountable embarrassments caused by the rotten sod. In fact, the only thing my grown-up rogue gene has not done is kill me! My guess is that from an early age it must have realised that that would be self-defeating. Kill me, kill my rogue gene.

So, for the time being anyway I have to battle on with life, manoeuvre over any ripples in space time disturbances engineered by my grown-up rogue gene and look forward to the day when I have to carry around a bag full of urine attached to my bladder via a catheter shoved up my penis, thereby preventing any kind of sex whatsoever. Even shower exercise! My wife won't be pleased with that.

Now, for those of you who didn't read my first book covering the period up to the time I left the army, titled MY ROGUE GENE, the book you are now reading is a sequel. A follow-on. It loosely describes some of the surprisingly stupid events that I've encountered from when I left the army in 1977 to the present time.

I say loosely because I have, again, embellished several of the incidents to disguise identities and make my life appear more interesting than it actually has been. So in keeping with my own protocol of secrecy I'll repeat what I told readers the first time...

'Characters, businesses, places, events and incidents could be the product of the author's imagination or might be used in a purely fictitious manner. Any resemblance to actual persons, living or dead, or actual events, may be purely coincidental.'

I hear you ask "Why write another book of inane yarns that show how grown-up rogue gene has influenced my life since leaving the army?"

Well, it's now been well over two years since the UK populace has enjoyed any kind of a normal existence because Covid keeps mutating and spreading, encouraged by lots of stupid people that insist on selfishly ignoring the mantra for getting vaccinated.

I don't know if you've noticed, but people really are stupid! You've only got to follow the politics of some countries, ours included, to realise that stupid people vote other stupid people into power, irrespective of any party that they support. Anyway that's, perhaps, a story for another time but right now, May 2022, we are still pestered by this insidious disease and we continue to wear face masks that mist up my spectacles every time I put one on.

So, with still more time on my hands and, indeed, while I'm still able I thought I would continue my homily to let you know what has happened to me since I left the army. A sweeping up exercise if you like, and because I've had time to cogitate over my previous book I've also inwardly recalled some more of the memories that were previously omitted and should have been included in that book. I'll try to slot these in now, if I can find a suitable opportunity to include them.

If you're not interested I don't care! Reflect on how much money you've wasted by buying this book, take it to the charity shop and get on with your life.

Also if, by any chance, you've read my previous book and you're now thinking to yourself "More bullshit," I don't care!

If you think my first book was a load of bullshit why have you gone out and bought this sequel? Stupid, or what?

Likewise, something I'm not going to do is mention any names. Some of the people cited have definitely died by now anyway. That's not my fault, that's their problem. However, when I describe an incident involving others and you think you recognise yourself, if you are still alive only you will know who you are, who was involved and what actually happened.

But there is an element of truth somewhere in the text... Isn't there?

Another thing... Be warned! I don't subscribe to the newsletter on political correctness. I believe in the philosophy of speaking what's obvious. Sheffield speak, where blokes are "blokes", women are "birds" and ugly people are, well... Ugly. So don't, therefore, be offended if I make any politically incorrect remarks. I'll try not to offend, but if you are offended, I don't care!

So this book is, again, about me. As I said, a continuance of my life since I left the army. It's definitely not an accurate biography. It's more a distorted recollection of events.

BOOK 1

COMMUNICATION

CHAPTER ONE

Bill's Sheffield Lingo

Before boring you with my anecdotes on employment I thought I would stroll along life's rich boulevard of communication.

Throughout one's life communication, as you know, plays an important role. However, my view is that communication with other people is fraught with danger and should be kept tightly locked away until it is absolutely essential that it be used. Don't do it. DO NOT communicate with anybody unless you have to. I mean it.

One only has to listen to the television or read the newspapers to realise what a mess people have got themselves into by, for example, communicating via social media... That is if you believe what you watch or what you read!

People have lost their jobs for tweeting or for using politically incorrect language. Politicians have lost votes and even had to resign because of some comment they made on Facebook or Twitter, some of these comments made years ago. Straightforward divorces have been complicated by the 'he said, she said' social media posts. Private and, indeed, personal photographs have been maliciously distributed worldwide without the owner's permission and some social media platforms are used for pornography. People have actually committed suicide because of the poisonous messages posted about them on social media!

Social media is invading all our lives and there is nothing we can do to curtail its relentless push to dominate our thoughts, opinions and personalities. Unless, of course, we all stop using it but I doubt that that suggestion will be taken seriously. To quote a phrase, 'We can't live with it but we can't live without it.'

Now, throughout my life I've been bugged by my rogue gene's persistent attempts to hinder and even curtail any progress or improvement I've tried to make. You'll therefore gather that despite my good intentions to be efficient and communicative I've spent most of my life struggling to make people understand me. You may recollect that I was born in Sheffield, Yorkshire, without doubt the centre of the Universe.

I think I may have already told you that but it does no harm to remind you.

Anyway, back in my very young days everyone understood each other perfectly. That's because nobody ever left the confines of Sheffield's boundaries and everyone in Sheffield spoke the same language. This lingo had a diction all of its own, and anyone visiting Sheffield had to be accompanied by a translator.

To explain this in more detail let's play a game. The idea of this game is that I give you a word or phrase and you have to guess what it means. I'll start with a couple of easy ones. Now don't cheat and look at the answers. They're at the end of this chapter...

1. "Eyup."
2. "Nowt."
3. "Gerroff!"
4. "Ooworriwee?
5. "Worriweeissen?"
6. "Tharonmifut!"
7. "Sumonemzgorragerroff."
8. "Midadsgorrajag."
9. "Eezgorrafacelikeabustedclogbottom."
10. "Eezdahnt'pub."
11. "Gissabuches."
12. "Tekitintut'ouwss."
13. "Shisgonnandunnit ageean."
14. "Gerrawaywithy."
15. "Thasnowtbutanit."
16. "Tekitaaht'saad. Now!"
17. "Naadendee. Wotdaahduin?"
18. "Gerrimineerwithi."

19. "Gissiteer."

20. "Wasak!"

I could go on for ages, but with dialect this baffling it's easy to see why people couldn't understand me when I got old enough to leave home and join the army.

For a long time after I had joined my army unit, at the age of fifteen, the only people who had an intelligent conversation in a group were blokes who came from Sheffield. And the Sheffielders were frequently put on 'showclean' for not speaking properly. Bloody rogue gene.

"Showclean?" I hear you ask. Army guys know what this is but for the benefit of you non-military personnel I'll explain.

We had to attend a parade of other showcleaners in best dress gear outside the guard room at 2000hrs on the evening we were put on showclean (that's eight p.m. to you non-military personnel). We had to take with us whatever it was that we were put on showclean for; unclean boots, unpressed trousers, unshaved chin, uncombed hair, etc., ensuring that we had put right what we had been put on showclean for. We were inspected by the Duty Officer. He had nothing else to do so it was a brief respite for him in the boredom of guarding the camp and it gave the bar steward time to prepare his nightcap.

The Sheffield bunch had to articulate from memory some obscure passage that we had to look up in the library. If we didn't articulate to the Duty Officer's satisfaction we were sent away to practice our passage and ordered to return at 2200hrs to recite the words again (that's ten o'clock in the evening for all you non-military personnel). We seldom had to return for a third attempt because the Duty Officer wanted to get to bed.

When I was a pupil at The Royal Military School of Music, Kneller Hall (KH) I was once told that Student Bandmasters with broad regional accents were sent for elocution lessons because broad regional accents were not permitted in front of an audience. 'One must speak the Queen's English while on the stage...' What the hell was 'Queen's English', anyway? I always thought that Sheffield lingo was the Queen's English.

Anyway, let's see how you faired with Sheffield lingo...

ANSWERS

1. Hello mate.
2. Nothing.
3. Leave it, it's mine. Get your own!
4. Who was he with?
5. Was he by himself?
6. You're on my foot and it hurts!
7. Some of those people have got to get off.
8. My father has just bought an up-market posh car with leather seats and wing mirrors.
9. He is ugly!
10. He's having a beer down at the pub.
11. Let's have a look at it, I'm a nosey sod.
12. Take it into the house.
13. She has gone and done the same thing again.
14. Get away with you, I don't believe it.
15. You are a stupid person.
16. Take it outside immediately, it stinks!
17. Now then, you. What do you think you're doing?
18. Get him in here with you.
19. Give it here, to me. It's mine.
20. Idiot ...*for a more detailed explanation you would benefit from reading my previous book*

Get the drift? Communication on this level takes practise unless you originate from Sheffield.

CHAPTER TWO

Bill's Cautious Answer

During my early army brainwashing days at Malta Barracks (the army called it 'induction & training'), communication with fellow soldiers sometimes got completely screwed up.

Take the time my platoon was being drilled on the square by our RSM. This guy had been through the wars. He had definitely been in a few fights at some time in his antiquity 'cos his face was really battered. His ears were cauliflower shaped, his crooked overhanging eyebrows seem to have been bashed into a neanderthal outcrop and his nose had been completely mashed. It had been pummelled so much the RSM couldn't resonate through his nose. Speaking, for him, was very much a blocked nose "I've got a bad cold" type of broadcast.

So, the RSM was vociferously drilling us. "LEFT, RIGHT, LEFT, RIGHT, LEFT, RIGHT, GET IT TOGETHER, LEFT, RIGHT, LEFT, RIGHT..."

Just as we were getting into the swing of things he abruptly brought us to a halt.

Now, here's a bit of information we found to be useful throughout our army careers; when a superior officer is shouting at you, you DO NOT look at him. Never, ever. Even if he stands in front of you, face-to-face, the end of his nose a fraction of an inch from yours you take on a vacant look in your eyes and stare through his head to the trees in the far distance.

You completely ignore the face staring at you. Making eye contact with a superior officer in some circumstances is tantamount to being insubordinate. So you look straight ahead and don't blink or move your eyeballs. Lock them into place.

Anyway, we stood to attention while the RSM approached us, each one of us a rigid steel column rooted to the spot. We knew he was going to speak to one of us by the way he was making a bee-line in our direction so we all stood there, feet firmly planted, waiting for his words of wisdom. He poked me in the chest with his pace stick.

"You! What's your name?"

"Pollard, sir."

"Where's your I.D. card?"

"In my left breast pocket, sir." That's the place where everyone's I.D. card should be kept.

"Get it out. Let me have it."

I retrieved my I.D. card from my pocket and handed it over.

"What's your number, Pollard?" he asked, scrutinising my I.D. card. Superior officers do this to make sure you know your army number. If you don't know your army number, you don't know who you are, so you don't exist in the eyes of the army.

I recite my army number. The RSM returned my I.D. card but I don't put it back in my pocket until given the all-clear. The RSM's face then gets close enough to mine for me to be able to tell what he had for breakfast and he asked, in a blocked nose menacing tone, "Am I ugly?"

Now this question is 'a rock and a hard place' probe. If I tell him he is ugly, which he undoubtedly is, he'll no doubt chastise me for being insubordinate. So I go for the polite response and answer, "No sir."

The RSM stepped back and roared to my neighbour,

"THAT MAN'S A LIAR. PUT HIM IN JAIL!" waving his pace stick about six inches from my face.

For ninety minutes grown-up rogue gene laughed while I was given the task of bulling both the Provo Sergeant's and the RSM's best boots (that's putting a glass like shine on them using spit and polish). Thinking about it I suspect that the RSM and Provo Sergeant had some kind of a deal going on to supply chumps like me for this very purpose, so no matter what I answered you can bet your jockstrap that I would have finished up in jail anyway.

The RSM released me when the drill session had finished, with a smile and a fatherly, "It pays to always tell the truth Pollard," and "You've done a good job on those boots."

A tick on rogue gene's list of successful covert operations.

CHAPTER THREE

Bill's Precarious Encounter

It is sometimes possible to antagonise someone else's rogue gene by acting the goat, especially with those in a position of power. Here's an example...

While I was on a violent and abusive body sculpturing fitness course called 'P' Company during my army days, a close friend of mine and I decided to take a shortcut to my car by walking across the square. We had to walk because we were too weak and battered to do anything else.

Now this was taboo! Honest. The square was for drilling (that's marching practise for you non-military personnel), for sweeping by the naughty boys, for parking your car on (providing you got permission from the RSM first), for parade rehearsal and for learning to drive (providing you got permission from the RSM first). The square was the RSM's domain and walking was definitely not in his vocabulary, and certainly not allowed on the square.

As we painfully sauntered towards my parked car we saw the RSM in the far distance, bent over and poking around in a gutter with his pace stick. At first my mate and I thought he might be clearing one of the drains of leaves but we kicked that idea into touch in the knowledge that the RSM would undoubtedly get some menial servant to do that job. He just wouldn't get the end of his pace stick dirty without a good reason but we couldn't guess what that was. Maybe he was trying to find something, his car keys or his wallet? Perhaps his loose change had fallen through a hole in his pocket... Doubtful 'cos his pocket had not been given permission to have a hole in it. Who knows what he was doing? RSM's lived in a world of their own.

At this point it's useful for you to know that our 'P' Company course took place in the middle of winter and on this particular day the wind was howling a gale across the square from the direction of the RSM towards my mate and me. The RSM had not yet noticed our gentle stroll.

As we walked, my mate must have had a cerebral aberration. 'P' Company, or something, must have made him snap. He stopped walking and looked at me with a smile that told me he was going to do something really bad. I swallowed hard in anticipation of what I didn't know was about to happen.

Turning towards the RSM my mate shouted, "Oi!"

Now "Oi!" is not how you address the RSM. Ever. It's just not a word he is familiar with. Not even his wife would dare to utter such a profanity at him. But with the wind howling in our direction it appeared that he hadn't heard what was shouted. He waved his arm dismissively at us as if to say "Get along with you."

So my mate decided to take things up a notch and shouted, "What are you doing, you prat!"

I turn to my mate and pleaded, "What are you doing? Are you f*****g mad?" to which he laughingly replied, "Watch this..."

The RSM stood there looking at us for a second, obviously trying to decipher what my mate had just said. He cups his hands to his mouth and shouts, "You what?"

My mate replies with a gibberish "Haawoathsmetonogerpaeqtp..."

The RSM repeats, "You what?" and again my mate sends back a mouthful of nonsense garbage "Haawoathsmetonogerpaeqtp..."

Deciding he's had enough of this verbal bantering, the RSM orders "Come 'ere, you two!" with his pace stick pointing to the space immediately in front of his boots. I feel a bit of jail time or at the very least millions of extra duties heading in our direction but my mate and I, nonetheless, make every effort to head towards the RSM in double time. Arriving in front of him we slam our tabs in, wait for his brain to engage and watch for his mouth to move.

"What was it you just said?"

In all seriousness my mate replied with, "Do you want any help, sir?"

My stomach tightened as I stifled a laugh. On close inspection my face might have given the game away, but the RSM had something else on his mind.

He actually smiled back. A pleasant, friendly smile. Not one of his more usual "I'm going to give you both hundreds of extra duties for wasting my time" smiles.

"That's very kind of you, boys," he said. "I've dropped my I.D. card.

Do you think you could find it for me?"

Another useful snippet of information... It is illegal, whilst in the army, to lose one's I.D. card. So the RSM may be feeling embarrassed about losing his... Perhaps.

We all searched the area, looking for the RSM's I.D. card, but to no avail. The wind must have taken it far away. After a about fifteen minutes of searching the RSM thanked us for our efforts and ordered us to "Fall out."

As we once more head towards my car, this time at a brisk pace in case the RSM was watching us, my mate suddenly stopped dead and slaps the flat of his foot on the concrete. Bending down he carefully peeled his shoe off the item he had just trapped under it.

"Look what I've found" he says, picking up the RSM's I.D. card with a smile.

We looked back at the RSM in the distance, head down still poking around in the leaves with his pace stick.

I asked, "Are you going to put him out of his misery?"

To which my mate responded, "Nah. Not yet. I'll let him stew for a while and I'll drop it into his office tomorrow."

As we got into my car I silently thought to myself, "Grown-up rogue gene didn't stand a chance against my mate."

CHAPTER FOUR

Bill's Convoy

I was once driving in a convoy that got lost.

Now, getting lost whilst in the army is not a good thing for morale, but in the final analysis there has to be scope for some laughs. Mind you, this unexpected incident happened at a time when magic gadgets had not yet been invented. Not even been thought of. There were no sat-navs, or mobile telephones that give you blisters on your swiping thumbs, or laptop computers, or Internet. To help drivers get from A to B all they had were inconveniently sized uncontrollable paper maps that were impossible to fold up. If you were rubbish at map reading you got lost.

It's true that the military did have radios to communicate with HQ, or the cookhouse, or the NAAFI, or your mate who had been posted abroad, but only those guys who had had extensive training were allowed to touch these wonders of technology.

Sit back and relax while I explain what happened.

The Battalion was out on exercise, probably somewhere cold and uncomfortable, but the band was back in camp rehearsing for nothing in particular. The Bandmaster (BM) got a call from the Military Transport (MT) section asking if the band had any spare bods. They were looking for someone to deliver some old Land Rovers to a handling unit in Tewkesbury, Gloucestershire, and to return in a new Land Rover for the Battalion. A long drive from Aldershot.

Myself and five other bandsmen with full driving licences were volunteered, one of us being a chap-in-charge Sergeant. We collected the Land Rovers from a central depot in Aldershot.

Now, a golden rule of convoy management is that the weakest, or slowest, vehicle should always be designated as the lead vehicle. The reason behind this is that if this vehicle decides to die, there will always be another to tow it to its final destination. So, after a briefing from the Officer signing the duff Land Rovers over to us we were taken to the yard holding the vehicles waiting to be collected. After a quick inspection of the vehicles our chap-in-charge Sergeant decided in his wisdom that he should be the lead vehicle driver. Not, as one would expect, in the weakest vehicle but in the cleanest, most reliable Land Rover on show. He gave specific instructions that we were not, under any circumstances, allowed to overtake him. The rest of us chose our vehicle, signed for the keys and documents and off we set on our long and boring drive to Tewkesbury.

With only one map between us we had huddled round the bonnet of the lead vehicle while our chap-in-charge Sergeant took us through the proposed route: from Aldershot to Cove, pick up the A327, north across the M3 motorway then north again to the M4 motorway. We would take a break on the M4 to have a drink and a sandwich and to review the map once more. The chap-in-charge Sergeant didn't exactly say at which service station, on the M4, we would stop. Just "The first one we come to."

So far so good.

The second rule of convoy management is that if you needed to communicate with the chap in front you should repeatedly flash him with your headlights. This flashing should be passed up the line to the lead vehicle who would then stop to find out what the problem was.

The final rule of convoy management is that if anyone in the convoy lost sight of the vehicle behind him he should pull over and stop to enable the missing vehicle to catch up. This philosophy would transmit up the line progressively until all the vehicles were, once more, a complete convoy.

With chap-in-charge Sergeant's reliable vehicle tearing away from us all the time he had to make frequent stops to enable the rest of the convoy to catch up. This frustrated him enormously.

During our briefing a suggestion that should have been made to us, but wasn't, was that it is advisable to memorise the number plate of the vehicle you are following. All Land Rovers looked exactly the same from the rear so without memorising this snippet of information you had no way of knowing who you should be following. This tip would prove to be of considerable use to us in the forthcoming hours of tedious motoring, if only we had thought of it.

So, any breakdowns in communication would create a scenario that one just could not expect to happen!

Our chap-in-charge Sergeant decided to ignore the fact that he was being followed and he pushed on. One can only think that chap-in-charge Sergeant assumed that number two driver would bring the rest of the convoy along the M4 to the first service station he would arrive at. The gap between him and number two vehicle increased with every red traffic light until he eventually disappeared from view.

*

Without a map, number two driver (not me – I was number three) stuck to the A327 towards the M4 motorway. However, unbeknown to number two, an unknown Land Rover had emerged from the army depot at Arborfield and turned left onto the A327 towards the M4... And this guy was on his way to deliver something to RAF Benson, near Wallingford in Oxfordshire, a far cry from Tewkesbury in Gloucestershire!

All Land Rovers look the same from behind, don't they?

Our number two came up behind this unidentified Rover at a red traffic light on the outskirts of Arborfield, but you don't need any prizes to guess what happened next. Yep, you've got it. He took it for granted that the unknown Rover was our lead vehicle driven by our chap-in-charge Sergeant because number two had not memorised chap-in-charge Sergeant's number plate. He religiously followed the vehicle in front of him... And the rest of the convoy religiously followed on behind number two!

Courtesy of John Creasey

*

Our chap-in-charge Sergeant, having eventually noticed that his convoy had evaporated from his rear view mirror, decided to pull into the first motorway service station on the M4 that he arrived at – Reading Services. He sat in the service station car park for an age assuming that his convoy would appear from the motorway slip road. After all, stopping at this service station was what he had told number two to do... Wasn't it? He was sure he had included this crucial instruction in his brief to the convoy drivers... Hadn't he?

He was now beginning to have doubts about that, and after dangling from the end of numerous cigarettes he walked up the services slip road to get a better view of the approach to this from the M4. Nope. Definitely no sign of the convoy. They should be here by now, surely?

Chap-in-charge Sergeant had a decision to make. Does he push on to Tewkesbury in the hopes that the convoy will catch up with him along the route (don't forget that they didn't have the map), or does he turn round at the next exit from the M4 and try to find his missing vehicles?

*

The convoy followed the Arborfield Land Rover as it turned left onto the M4. Oddly, the lead vehicle, supposedly driven by chap-in-charge Sergeant or so number two thought, turned off the M4 sooner than anticipated and drove north along the A33 to later join the A329 towards Wallingford. We all thought, "Didn't chap-in-charge Sergeant say that they would call in at a motorway service station?" Ah well, maybe he changed his mind. That's what chap-in-charge Sergeants do isn't it, change their minds?

*

Chap-in-charge Sergeant decided that the best plan was to continue along the agreed route to Tewkesbury, this time at a much slower speed, in the hope that the convoy would catch him up. Along the M4 he was constantly abused by car horns reminding him that the upper speed limit was 70mph, not the 35mph he was sticking to! Lorry drivers coming up behind him didn't hesitate to give him an ear bashing, with lots of unsavoury hand signals and fist waving as they had to wait for a slot in the traffic to overtake him. The slow speed created a mile-long traffic tailback of frustrated drivers, with madmen weaving in-and-out of the motorway lanes to get somewhere quicker than the rest of the drivers.

As if chap-in-charge Sergeant's rogue gene had not had enough fun at his expense an opportunity arose that just could not be missed. A police car sidled up alongside chap-in-charge Sergeant's Rover and the cop in the passenger seat signalled for him to pull over. With nowhere else to go chap-in-charge Sergeant pulled onto the hard shoulder and rolled to a stop. Motorways had hard shoulders in those days, intended for emergency breakdowns.

The cops exited their car and approached chap-in-charge Sergeant who was, by now, stood next to his vehicle.

"Good morning, sir. Are you having any problems with your vehicle?"
"Er, no. Not exactly."
"So what, exactly, is the reason you are in danger of creating an accident by driving so slowly?"
"Well..." a pause while chap-in-charge Sergeant thought about a plausible answer, "...my convoy is missing."

The cops looked at each other, then back to chap-in-charge Sergeant.

"So you've lost a convoy. Is that it, sir?"

"Well, no... I haven't exactly lost the convoy, they just haven't caught up with me yet."

"Would you like to expand on that, sir?" a puzzled look on the cop's face.

"Not really, but I'll try to explain."

In some discomfort chap-in-charge Sergeant explained the situation about losing his convoy, much to the amusement of the cops.

"I think you had better follow us to the next intersection where we can decide what to do about finding your convoy," instructed the policeman. "We'll radio for some assistance while we are on our way."

Chap-in-charge Sergeant was now in a different convoy. One that he didn't expect to be in.

*

After about forty-five minutes the convoy I was in, the one following a nameless Rover, arrived at RAF Benson. The convoy drivers all followed the 'lead' vehicle through the gates of the airfield and to its MT shed. We all exited from our vehicles and looked at each other with baffled faces. This guy didn't look anything like our chap-in-charge Sergeant.

The nameless 'lead' driver came over to us.

"Do you guys know where you're going?"

"We know where we should be going, but we're not too sure we're on the right track," my mate answered.

"Oh? Where are you supposed to be going?"

My mate explained about our mission to deliver our Rovers to Tewkesbury and then turned to number two.

"Why the f*** did you follow this guy?" pointing to the stranger.

"I thought he was Sergeant {Name}."

"What? He doesn't look anything like {Name}!"

"I know that now, but I didn't know that when we joined him at Arborfield," looking more surprised than any of us.

Number two explained how he had lost chap-in-charge Sergeant and then "thought he had found him" when he pulled up at the red traffic light way back in Arborfield. We couldn't help but smile at this unintended misdirection and we decided on a plan to get us back on track.

With the help of the stranger one of us would go to the MT office, get a map and then get back on the road. No need to disturb anyone official with this, 'cos we were confident that we could get to Tewkesbury without any more problems. We voted in a new chap-in-charge of the lead vehicle and agreed a system of communication in case we needed it. We also agreed it was a good idea to memorise the number plate in front of us... It's never too late to learn, is it?

The convoy left the airfield without being stopped. We all breathed a sigh of relief at that and continued up the A4047 towards the A34 and then onto the A40 towards Cheltenham. Tewkesbury wasn't far away from Cheltenham.

*

Chap-in-charge Sergeant followed the police car to the next M4 intersection. Turning off the motorway they parked up in a layby just outside Theale. The policeman was still on his radio talking to some distant traffic controller.

"I've put a call out to see if we can find your missing convoy," the cop advises. "We'll give it about half-an-hour to see if the convoy appears somewhere on route."

After half-an-hour of chatting and smoking cigarettes his convoy wasn't discovered so chap-in-charge Sergeant decided to get back on the road after an ear bashing and a few choice words of advice about the perils of travelling so slowly on the motorway.

A specific meeting point on route to Tewkesbury was agreed, just in case the convoy was intercepted somewhere.

*

The convoy didn't have any more hiccups. With an uneventful journey it was able to get a good head of steam up on the A40 towards Cheltenham. From there they joined the M5 motorway towards Tewkesbury.

*

Chap-in-charge Sergeant also had an uneventful journey, turning off the M4 onto the A419 then along the A417 at Cirencester towards Gloucester. The A417 intersects the M5 on the way to Gloucester and once on this motorway chap-in-charge Sergeant also had the opportunity to get some steam up.

After about five minutes he charged across the A40 intersection and guess what? Up ahead he eyeballed a convoy of Land Rovers! The question is, was it his convoy? Pressing the pedal to the metal he steamed up the motorway until he was able to overtake the tail-ender.

Levelling up with the driver's window he peered across and recognised the tail-end driver. The tail ender took on a baffled look as he thought to himself, "Where the hell did he spring from?"

With a sigh of relief chap-in-charge Sergeant started to accelerate to the front of the convoy. However, the current convoy leader saw this Rover charging up the centre lane of the motorway and assumed it was one of the other convoy drivers playing games, so he also accelerated to maintain his leadership. Everyone else followed.

The convoy was now travelling well in excess of the permitted sixty m.p.h. for military convoys and the two leaders were still playing a mad game of 'catch-me', one driver trying to lead the convoy and the other not willing to give up his leadership... If only he knew who had just re-joined the convoy! Nobody knew the actual speed the convoy was travelling 'cos everybody was concentrating on keeping a straight trajectory without smashing into the vehicle in front.

It never rains but it pours, doesn't it? Everyone heard the sound of a police siren charging up the motorway towards the convoy. A glance in all mirrors confirmed a police car, blue lights and main beams flashing, rapidly approaching the Land Rovers. Chap-in-charge Sergeant eased out of the centre lane into the convoy and started flashing his own headlights to signal the lead vehicle to pull over and stop. All Rovers came to a stop on the hard shoulder as the police car swerved in front of the lead vehicle.

We all exited from our rides and waited for the policeman to approach us. Chap-in-charge Sergeant was giving us a proper ear bashing, calling us all unmentionable names and threatening all sorts of harsh penalties for 'getting lost'. The policeman puffed his chest out and strode up to us.

"Good morning gents. Which one of you is busting to go to the toilet?"

We all stood there waiting for someone to answer up.

"Let me see your licenses and I.D. cards," the policeman instructs, holding out his hand. We took out our driving licenses and I.D. cards and handed them over to the cop.

Chap-in-charge Sergeant pipes up, "Is there a problem, officer?"

"Well, that depends on why you were exceeding the speed limit. You are aware that military convoys are restricted to sixty m.p.h., aren't you?"

"Yes. Were we going faster than that?" An innocent look on chap-in-charge Sergeant's face. All the convoy drivers looked round at each other with a look of surprise on their faces, holding the palms of their hands up in submission.

"Yes, sir. Seventy seven m.p.h."

"Nooo... Surely not that fast."

"Yes, sir. Seventy seven."

"Well, we're taking these Land Rovers to Tewkesbury to get them exchanged because the speedometer is faulty on all of them."

"Is that right, sir..." A pause as the policeman compared our I.D. cards with each of our licenses.

"We've received a message that a convoy of Land Rovers is lost. That's not you, by any chance, is it?"

"Absolutely not, officer."

Chap-in-charge produced the paperwork associated with the exchange of vehicles. After a detailed inspection the policeman handed back our documents with some stern words of warning about speeding and instructions that none of us were permitted to overtake him while we travelled up the M5 to our turn-off on the A46 to Ashchurch, where the army camp was situated. On approach to the A46 the police car pulled onto the hard shoulder and the officer pushed his arm out of the window to wave us on. We joined the road to Ashchurch and continued our journey.

Arriving at the camp we located the MT shed and parked our vehicles. An Officer, a Lieutenant, emerged from a door in the building and approached us as we all prepared our documents for hand-over.

"Hello, chaps. You're a little later than anticipated but you're here now so we'll get on with this hand-over." As we walked to the MT shed the Officer passed the time of day by casually talking to chap-in-charge Sergeant.

"We've had reports of a missing convoy somewhere down south," with a laugh. "Can't have been you lot 'cos you're here..."

"Some idiot must have been leading that convoy," offers chap-in-charge Sergeant to a volley of agreeing "Yea" from the rest of us.

"A convoy has also been pulled over on the M5 for speeding. That wasn't by any chance you lot, was it?"

"No sir. Our journey from Aldershot has been quiet. If anything it was boring. Absolutely no problems at all..."

I reckon my grown-up rogue gene, and perhaps a few other people's grown-up rogue genes, had a good time with that one!

CHAPTER FIVE

Bill's Wedding

Sometimes communication can be expressed by actions, not words.

With a couple of mates I once gate-crashed a wedding in Cyprus. The intrusion to the couple's happiest moment was purely accidental. We didn't intend to gate-crash the gathering, we just found ourselves being welcomed to a feast that was laid out on tables that had been set up to completely block off a narrow street in Limassol. Limassol is a completely different town now, but back in the day our barracks were situated on the hill overlooking it, a twenty minute walk or a five minute taxi ride from the camp.

Talking about the taxi ride from Limassol reminds me of an evening when a mate of mine and I visited our favourite bar for a few drinks.

Everyone in the Battalion had a favourite bar in Warrior Square, the red light district of Limassol, and we all stood by our unwritten agreement that what goes on abroad, during our overseas postings, stays abroad.

At each and every visit to our favourite bar we were always plied with a few free drinks by a gorgeous hostess to loosen us up for "something extra" if it was requested. Now, this "something extra" varied in scope depending on how much one was prepared to pay. I think you know what I allude to. Anyway, my mate was conscious of the fact that it was his turn to pay for the taxi home (I had paid for the taxi to town), and he asked me to hang on to his ten-bob taxi fare in case his "desire" emptied his wallet. I put the ten-bob note in my top pocket and waited patiently for his desire to be curbed.

Ironically, after his promotion this same 'mate' knifed me in the back during the latter days of my army career. The lesson, here, is that no matter how close you think a friendship is to you, promotion always eradicates any trace of that bond...

On another occasion a different mate of mine had emptied his wallet while in Warrior square and had to walk back to camp.

I forgot to mention that about two hundred metres from our camp was another barracks, this one holding a battalion of Greek soldiers. Not one to waste energy, and in true military fashion anyway, my mate drunkenly decided to take a direct-line route to his bed in our camp, a route that inevitably took him through the middle of the Greek barracks because this was in a straight line from Limassol to our camp.

Like a guided missile he trudged up the hill to the Greek camp's main gate, manned by a couple of guards. Despite their protestations my mate continued through the Greek's quarters, nervously accompanied by reinforcements from that camp's guardroom. On reaching the rear gate the guards at that location obligingly opened the gate to let him depart.

From that time onwards each and every occasion that my mate got drunk and had to walk back to his bed he took the same direct route home... And he was waived through by the Greek guards! He knew where he was going, they knew where he was going and they also knew that he was no threat to them unless, that is, anyone tried to stop him...

Anyway, I digress. I was going to explain how I had become involved in gate-crashing a wedding, wasn't I? Firstly, though, I need to describe the events leading up to that intrusion.

We had been posted to Cyprus as a contingent of the United Nations Forces In Cyprus (UNFICYP). Some of my time in Cyprus was discussed in my previous book. Did you buy that book? If not, you missed out on a lot of my whacky anecdotes. Your loss...

So, each year towards the end of the summer Limassol's ruling council organised the Limassol Wine Festival, when all the wine producers of Cyprus were invited to set up a stall in the centre of Limassol to peddle their wares. It was a good opportunity to tell the country, and the world at large, what a good grape growing season they had had, and what good vino the producers had fermented for our pleasure.

I and most of the Battalion went down to the town to investigate, ignoring the fact that the Festival had trespassed across our favourite bar in Warrior Square. In fact, all the bars had been closed so that the bar owners could enjoy themselves at the Festival... And enjoy themselves they did!

The Festival was one huge party that went on for days until all the gallons of wine on display had been guzzled, vomited up, guzzled some more and eventually consumed in its entirety. The wine producers provided a limitless, never-ending supply of vino for everyone attending this party to smell, taste and spit out using the copious supply of buckets scattered around each display to catch the discharge. In fact, the buckets were rarely emptied because they rarely got full... Most people just swallowed their vino!

The wine was free. You could go from one stall to the next pouring wine down your throat from the plastic cups provided by the vendor. The original idea, I presume, was that you dribble a few drops of wine into the cup, smell it, sip it and then spit it out. By the time my mates and I arrived any notion of a delicate wine tasting had died by the wayside and the locals were helping themselves to oodles of the stuff to drink there and then. If one liked a particular wine that one came across in this melee of guzzling, wine-spilling, back-slapping, congratulating and vomiting one could purchase a plastic demijohn for two Cypriot shillings and refill this as many times as one liked... Absolutely free! No holds barred, no questions asked.

We welcomed this philosophy and spent the whole day aimlessly wandering around the Festival, slowly getting smashed.

So what did this raucous, boozy gathering have to do with us gate-crashing a wedding?

Well, we decided that our boozy session needed a meal to soak up the vino. That way we could slosh more wine before getting paralytic and legless. So we went looking for a restaurant... But all the restaurants were closed for the festival, weren't they? Nonetheless, we searched as many side-streets as we could find in the hopes that we would happen on a restaurant that was open. We didn't find one but we did come across a noisy street party.

A bloke stood up from his seat at the table and approached us.

"What have you brought?" he asked.

My quick-thinking mate held up his demijohn and replied, "More wine."

My other mate and I both held our demijohns high in unison.

The party guest turned to the table in glee and shouted, "Reinforcements!" He then pulled my elbow towards the party with, "Come. Come and join us."

With all manner of food covering every table how could we refuse? Chairs appeared from a house and we were slotted in between some gorgeous looking women who made all three of us extremely welcome. We were all introduced to the bride and groom and given a bear hug and a kiss on our cheeks from both of them.

On returning to camp one of my mates crowed about how one of the two women that flanked him at the table kept squeezing his thigh, though he had to admit that this had had little effect because he was too smashed to appreciate it. My other mate crowed about how he had enjoyed the bride clutching the cheeks of his arse during his introduction bear hug!

Anyway, we stayed with the wedding party for the rest of the day and long into the night. When asked we took it in turns to return to the Festival with about twenty other blokes to refill the party's demijohns. We had a great time, with fantastic hosts, delicious food, a limitless supply of vino and lots of dancing with a whole range of Cypriot women, from the huge and wobbly grandmas to five year old grand-kids. They just never stopped eating, drinking, singing, dancing and being merry. Much to everyone's amusement my mates and I even took part in a competition to see who was best at dancing the Kartzilamas, a really lively affair where men dance in pairs across from each other to demonstrate their virility and agility. Neither I nor any of my mates won... We found it extremely difficult to even stand upright!

At about twelve thirty a.m. my mates and I had had enough. As we retrieved our berets from the heads of blokes who had collapsed under their table our host begged us to stay.

"You cannot go yet," he demands, "you will miss the coupling celebration."

"Coupling celebration? What's that?" I ask.

"You must stay to see," he replies with enthusiasm, removing my beret and skimming it Frisbee style to one of the kids.

So we decided to drink some more, dance some more and chat about nothing in particular. We didn't have to wait long.

At twelve forty-five the bride and groom rose from their chairs and, with much cheering and raising of glasses, they made their way hand in hand to one of the homes adjacent to the party tables. As soon as they disappeared inside everything went quiet. The silence was deafening. I turned to our host to ask why everyone was just sitting at their table motionless, as if their life spring had just wound down, but before I could speak he brought his index finger to his lips in a sign for me to keep quiet. Nobody moved. Not even the children who had been ordered to "sit there, keep quiet and don't move." Any suggestion of a movement towards one's glass for a drink was met with a steely reprimanding stare from the bride's father. Deathly silence.

My mates and I were beginning to get a little uncomfortable as we eyed each other and watched the party guests staring at their hands or their opposite number or their plate of crumbs waiting to be replenished with another bread bun.

After about ten minutes of this unsettling silence we heard a noise. It was the noise of a window being opened. Everyone looked upwards to the opened window, a sense of anticipation spreading through the guests at the table. It was as if everyone was on a knife-edge. My mates and I looked at each other, wide-eyed and ready to spring into action if anything sinister happened, hearts pounding at the tenseness of the situation.

A white sheet appeared out of the open window and was draped over the sill by an unseen person. A tiny speckle of blood on the sheet was barely visible. Everyone in the street downstairs suddenly burst into a raucous, joyous cheer with lots of back slapping, hand shaking, fist pumping and arm waving. Several of the women started to sob into lace hankies and the men refilled their glasses and raised these in celebration.

With a look of surprise my mates and I joined in the applause and our host beckoned us over to a quiet corner.

"Do you see what happened?" he asked with a broad smile and glee in his eyes.

"Yea...?" we questioned with a nod and a look of puzzlement.

"Let me explain," the host proffers. "Here in Cyprus we have a tradition at weddings that communicates whether the bride and groom have consummated their marriage. When they left the table it is incumbent upon all the guests to provide them with as much privacy as possible. Hence our silence. Now, if the marriage has been properly consummated the bride hangs her bloodied sheet out of the window to let everyone know that there is no problem with her husband's love making, so the marriage is destined to last. If, however, the bride displays a clean sheet it is a sign that the marriage has not been consummated and she returns to collect her belongings, then leaves the party with her guests. That would be a very sad thing because tradition has it that the marriage will fail, so you see how important it is to give the bride and groom some privacy."

"What if the bride is not a virgin?" asked my mate.

The other mate pops in with, "Supposing there is no blood?"

The host continued, "We live in a progressive society. If that is the case it is acceptable for the groom to prick his finger... Providing they both agree that consummation has been successful. After all, nobody really believes that the bride is a virgin nowadays, although it is expected by many parents even today."

"Have you ever seen a situation where the marriage has not been consummated?"

"Never..."

I always find it amazing how people stick to tradition. Even though they no longer believe in it.

CHAPTER SIX

Bill Farting

Let's move on a pace and look at communication post army.

Before I delve into this whiffy subject I thought I'd ask just one question. Who, among you, are embarrassed by farting? Not just you, yourself farting but hearing someone else's fart.

Well you shouldn't be. It's a perfectly natural thing to do. It's biologically inevitable. Impossible to prevent. All that food that you shovel down your throat is dissolved by your gastric juices, broken down into its component parts, and distributed around your body in the form of sugars that give you energy or, if you're anything like me, makes you fat.

In reality, I'm fat because my body is stupid enough not to realise that the food I empty down my throat is converted to sugars that I don't actually need, 'cos I don't need it in the form of energy for running, cycling, weight lifting or doing any other activity with a propensity to make me fatigued. I had enough of those games while I was in the army.

So my body stupidly stores these sugars in the form of fat, just in case I do need some energy at some time in the future. But I doubt that I will. To quote a figurative phrase, "fat chance... "

However, the end result of this bodily function is to produce waste in the form of sausage-like entities that you drop into some water at the bottom of a toilet pan and flush away... Turds, together with waste gas that builds up inside your large intestine and stretches this until it forces its way out of your arse. Farts vibrate your sphincter and make a sound not dissimilar to a car without an exhaust pipe. Sometimes they smell...

Cows fart. They're apparently damaging the ozone with their farts. Dogs fart and when they fart it stinks! Dog farts will clear a room quicker than you can swat a fly! I've never heard a cat fart. But I do know that fish fart 'cos I've seen the bubbles rise. And I know for a fact that people fart because they leave it loitering behind them and move on to the bread section in the supermarket.

Every living thing farts. It happens. It's natural. It's unavoidable. So get over it, get used to it and move on. Wait 'till you get to my age. Then you'll accept farting as an inevitable consequence of growing old.

The point I'm trying to make is that sometimes you don't need to use your vocal chords to communicate. Your sphincter will do just as good a job.

I recollect a time when I was a suit (i.e. I worked in an office and wore a suit). The office that I inhabited was on the middle floor of a three storey building. The gent's toilet for the whole building was located on my floor so the poor saps that worked on the other two floors had to travel a bit to use the gents. Too bad for them if they got the 'Tangier Trots' after a night on the curry. However, being on different floors the blokes rarely met inside this particular social club unless they'd had too much to drink at lunchtime or had eaten some bad sushi.

Anyway, there were three cubicles in our gent's toilet.

During one of my trips to the toilet to expel some of the morning's breakfast I found the only available cubicle was the centre one, the other two having been occupied just prior to my visit. In silence I locked the door, lowered my trousers, lowered my underpants and lowered myself to prepare for a few minutes of quiet contemplation. The silence was deafening.

With my elbows on my thighs and my head in my hands I was lost in deep contemplative thought, trying to think of ways to improve my downtrodden destiny. After several minutes I heard the bloke in the cubicle on my right take a deep breath. Suddenly the whole room shook as he farted. A massively long, loud fart that made all the doors and windows rattle in their frames.

"BBBRRRRRRRRRRRRRRRRRRRRRUP!"

I sat there, trying not to make a sound as my shoulders gigged up and down in silent hand-over-my-mouth laughter.

After a few more moments of quiet stillness the bloke in the cubicle on my left decided to respond with an earth vibrating rumbling fart of his own that almost cracked the toilet pan.

"BBBRRRRRRRRRRRRRRRRRRRRRUP!"

I almost fell off the toilet seat, trying hard not to let the other guys know how hilarious the stereo effect had been inside my own cubicle. In fact the strain of holding my chuckles to myself created a pressure on my bowels that forced a long loud fart from my own arse.

"BBBRRRRRRRRRRRRRRRRRRRRRUP!"

After a silent pause the guy on my right said, "who asked you to butt in?"

The guy on my left immediately concurred with, "Yea. This is a private conversation."

In fits of laughter we finished what we were doing, dressed ourselves and stood in front of our sinks to wash our hands. Nobody said a word. Nobody needed to.

We just looked at each other and smiled before leaving the toilet to get on with some more tedious nine-to-five tasks.

CHAPTER SEVEN

Bill's Insurance Howlers

One of my many employment positions was with an insurance company.

I was employed as a Technical Adviser and one of my tasks was to answer complaints or queries from people who had taken out an insurance policy with this company. I had to answer some extraordinary phone calls.

"You have changed my little boy into a little girl. Will this make any difference?" Or,

"Sir, I am glad to say that my husband that was reported missing is now dead." Or,

"The indirect cause of the accident was a little guy in a small car with a big mouth."

Can you imagine just how much fun my rogue gene had while I'm on the telephone trying to sort out this type of conversation? It made sure that I sometimes had to spend ages with a claimant to get to the bottom of what happened... And my boss rarely believed my report.

Now, over the years I've collected lots of such conversations from many varied sources. From work, from the internet, from friends and from my travels.

Here's a few of my favourites...

- "Mrs A had no clothes, had not had any for some time. The clergy have been visiting her."
- "I am forwarding my marriage certificate and two children, one of which is a mistake you made."
- "I am riting (sic) these lines for Mrs B who cannot rite (sic) herself. She expects to be confined next week and can do with it."
- "Milk is needed for the baby and father is unable to supply it."
- "In answer to your question, I have given birth to a little boy weighing ten pounds. Is this satisfactory?"
- "I want money as quickly as you can send it. I have been in bed with the doctor for a week and he doesn't seem to be doing me any good."

- "Re your dental enquiry, the teeth in the top are all right, but the ones in my bottom are hurting terribly."
- "In accordance with your instructions, I have given birth to twins in the enclosed envelope."
- "My car was legally parked as it backed into the other vehicle."
- "An invisible car came out of nowhere, struck my car and vanished."
- "The guy was all over the road. I had to swerve a number of times before I hit him."
- "I saw a slow-moving, sad-faced old gentleman as he bounced off my windscreen."
- "The pedestrian had no idea which way to run, so I ran over him."
- "I was on my way to the doctor with rear end trouble when my universal joint gave way, causing me to have an accident."
- "I was sure the old fellow would never make it to the other side of the road when I struck him."

There is little wonder that I believe in the philosophy of keeping quiet.

So, the moral of this entire section on communication is "stay well away from communication with other people!" It provides fodder for your grown-up rogue gene to feed on and it makes life extremely complicated.

BOOK 2

EMPLOYMENT

CHAPTER EIGHT

Bill Signing On

November 1977

Civvy employment... Phuh! I've got about ten T-shirts of civvy employment history.

I never thought I would be jobless so early in my life. I was really counting on being a Student at The Royal Military School Of Music, Kneller Hall at this particular time in my life, but unfortunately my grown-up rogue gene had other ideas. That bloody obnoxious entity had engineered a stormy period in my army career and I found it necessary to hand in my notice. I left the army full of disappointment and anger. There were now several people topping my list of arrogant backstabbers who I prayed I would never meet in the street.

So, I've departed from the army, departed from Aldershot and I'm now living with my mother-in-law in Worcester Park, Surrey. All the personal contents from my army quarter are stored in the garage at the bottom of the garden. Not an ideal place to store furniture 'cos it's cold, it's damp and it's probably easily accessed by all kinds of rodents and creatures. I'll probably return to these to find that they have all been chewed up to be used for nesting material. Still, it's better than nothing. I couldn't afford proper commercial storage 'cos I haven't found a job yet and most of my savings had been taken up with me buying out of the army.

It could have been a bad call leaving the army with just ten weeks left for my twelve years in service and a free pass on leaving, but if I'd stayed any longer I could see myself getting into deep trouble with my hostile attitude towards certain personnel.

I hadn't, in my opinion, been treated fairly by the army so I left under a dark cloud. You'll have to read my previous book for a more detailed description of events, but suffice to say that I was crapped on in a big way. Probably the accomplishment of my younger rogue gene provoked, no doubt, by the self-importance and arrogance of a few people that I left behind.

No point in chuntering on about it now. It's time to look forward to a new life. A different life. A life that I alone could control. Not a life of following someone else's demands and orders... Apart from my wife's, or so I thought. For a while I temporarily forgot about my rogue gene because I had other things to concentrate on. Like finding a job and finding somewhere permanent to live. My dad kept on about joining a Union but I had decided to give a miss to anything resembling an army, and a Union was deemed by me to definitely resemble an army. Rules, regulations and people pretending to be in charge. My army resettlement board had been about as useful as an empty egg timer, so I was on my own with regards to employment.

I went to sign on at the local Labour Exchange, now referred to as the Employment Office.

This turned out to be an open plan office filled with cheap plastic chairs in numerous rows facing a couple of desks. Behind the rows of chairs was a pin board covering the width of the room. On this was pinned a selection of available jobs from local employers.

Getting numb-bum I decided to see what was on offer, but I didn't want to lose my place in this lengthy queue. I asked the guy sat next to me if he would mind keeping my place for me. He seemed an obliging chap and his smiling affirmative response gave out a trustworthy impression.

Rising from my seat I went over to the pin board, rubbing some feeling back into my buttocks.

There must have been fifty or sixty jobs on offer. Keeping an eye on the queue for an interview at one of the desks I scanned the postcards pinned to the board. Nothing of interest. Plenty of vacancies for office cleaners, couriers (with their own bike), burger flippers, bed makers, street sweepers, dustbin collectors, window cleaners, dish washer uppers, etc. Nothing for a draftsman.

Why did I want a job as a draftsman? Well, I'd just spent almost twelve years as a trombone player in the army and I had decided that there wasn't much call for a trombone player in civvy street unless one was famous, which I wasn't. So I thought back to what I enjoyed most at school. Technical drawing. I'd had this ridiculous conversation with the chaps on my army resettlement board, during which they tried everything to persuade me to go back into uniform. But they struck out so I stuck to my plan of being a draftsman after getting myself settled into my own civvy uniform of jeans, t-shirt and trainers.

Seeing nothing of interest on the pin board I pivoted to return to my seat. Everyone in the queue had moved up a couple of chairs and lo and behold, mine was now occupied by a sniffing, scruffy looking long haired youth who didn't seem as if he'd had a bath for about a year. He certainly hadn't used the soap dispenser attached to the wall by the entrance door. I walked up to him.

"That's my seat."

"No it isn't. You left it ages ago."

"No, I left it three minutes ago to look at the job vacancies."

"Well it was empty, so I took it."

"Well how about you 'un-take' it and let me sit down?"

"Get lost!"

I thought about helping this guy lose his consciousness, but then thought better of it. After all it probably wouldn't have made my job search any easier, would it? Anyway my chair would, by now, probably be infested with fleas or crabs or E. Coli or something just as nasty!

I turned to the now untrustworthy guy I'd asked to save my seat.

"I thought you were going to save my seat?"

"I forgot."

"You forgot? It was only about three minutes ago that you promised to save that chair for me."

"I forgot."

Is this what it's like out in Civvy Street? Every man for himself? No honour? No reliability? It reminded me of certain army personnel that were now at the top of my list of people to hate.

I decided to wait until it would have been Mr Untrustworthy's turn to approach the desk, then step in front of him before he reached it. That would teach him to be more trustworthy.

I stood to one side of the rows of chairs until I heard the magic word "next!" and started my walk towards the desk. Mr Untrustworthy second guessed me, jumped up and made haste in the same direction as me. I accelerated. He accelerated. We met about three yards from the desk and tried to elbow each other out of the way as we headed in the direction of the waiting interviewer. We both arrived at the same time and hustled over the waiting chair, as if taking part in a game of musical chairs when the music stops.

With a look of exasperation the interviewer says, "Who's next?"

Mr Untrustworthy and I both spoke up in unison, "I am."

The interviewer looked up at both of us and asked Mr Untrustworthy, "What's your number?"

With a slightly furrowed brow I thought, "Number? What number...?"

Mr Untrustworthy, "245."

Interviewer, looking in my direction, "What's your number?"

Me, "Er..., don't have one."

Interviewer, pointing to the entrance, "Didn't you pick one up on your way in?"

I turned to follow the direction of his finger. Staring at me from the entrance door, I now realise, was not a soap dispenser but a ticket dispenser with a long slither of paper dropping from its arse.

I thought, "Oh, Shit... " and turned back to the desk.

Interviewer, "First time here?" looking sympathetic.

"Yea... "

"I'm afraid you'll have to go get a number and then re-join the queue."

Mr Untrustworthy smiled. As I turned to go back to the soap dispenser for a ticket I saw the flea infested drop-out also smiling. That's two people on my list of 'to see to' if we met outside.

***

I took my ticket from the machine, number 440, and sat on the end of the row furthest from the desks to await my turn. This time I'm not going anywhere except down the line to my turn for an interview.

Two and a half hours later I was back in front of the desks.

"Next!"

At last...

I took my seat in front of the interviewer. The same one that made me go back for a number. This was a bit disappointing 'cos I just knew that this guy was a 'jobsworth'. I knew that because I'd just met him two and a half hours ago.

"How can I help you?"

"I need to sign on for unemployment benefit."

"Oh, really? Why's that?"

"Because I'm unemployed."

"I figured that, but why are you unemployed?"

"I've just left the army and... "

"Ah," he interrupts. "I'll need to get a different form for you. Wait there for a couple of minutes?"

What else could I do? I certainly wasn't going to give up this chair to anyone, having waited so long to get this far. I nodded in agreement.

The interviewer got up and left the room. I looked around, as one does, while I waited for him to return. A chap from India sat down in front of the adjacent desk with a broad ultra-white smile occupying his face. I know he was from India because I heard him say so to his interviewer.

Earwigging his conversation I gleaned that he had arrived in Britain a mere three days ago, he was homeless with his wife and eight kids, he was jobless and he was desperate for some free money.

The interviewer took on an optimistic tone and gave the Indian guy some hope for a more comfortable life.

"I'm confident that I can help. Do you have a bank account?"

"Yes."

"What...?" I thought, "In the country for three days and he's already got a bank account? He didn't waste any time did he?"

I've had my name on the bank's list of 'things to look into' for ten days and I still haven't heard when, or even if, the Worcester Park branch will transfer my account from the Aldershot branch!

After asking several questions concerning the guy's circumstances the interviewer listed the benefits he could provide to this cheerful chap from our Commonwealth partner. There was twenty pounds for this, twenty-five pounds for that, fifteen pounds for something else, and several more benefits that an immigrant of this guy's status could be provided with. Tallying the list, the interviewer offered the guy about eighty pounds per week, a sum enthusiastically accepted by him. Eighty pounds per week doesn't sound a lot today, but back in 1977 it was a small fortune.

He was also put on the housing list for a council house, with a promise to find him a roof over his head within three weeks. Not that he needed one, anyway, 'cos he was staying with a cousin.

Listening to this conversation, and hearing the outcome, I was infused with hope. A sum like that would certainly help me in my struggle to integrate with my civvy street community.

My own interviewer returned to his seat with a new questionnaire, provoking my rogue gene into action.

I was, essentially, asked exactly the same questions as my Indian neighbour.

Was I classed as an immigrant?

After a lengthy discussion on my circumstances the interviewer cheerfully advised me about my own benefits.

"I can authorise a benefit for you, Mr Pollard. That will be Unemployment Benefit, with a government grant of nine pounds and forty-five pence per week... "

"Uuuuh... ?" I thought to myself, "Is he taking the piss?"

With a sense of disappointment I reasoned, "That guy's been in this country for just three days and he's been offered eighty quid a week. I'm in exactly the same situation as he is!" I plead, pointing to the Indian chap and his wife departing from the room with three of his kids bringing up the rear. One of the kids was trailing a long strip of tickets being pulled out of the room from the soap dispenser's arse. The number from that machine must now be in the thousands!

I continue to plead my case.

"I'm homeless with a wife and two kids, I'm jobless and I need more than nine pounds and forty-five pence per week to tide me over until I can find a job."

"Well, you're not exactly homeless are you? You're living with your mother-in-law."

"He's living with his cousin," pointing my thumb over my shoulder.

"I know, but he's only just arrived in the country."

"So what? Suppose Mum-in-law decides to ask for some rent? How about you put me on the housing list?"

"Do you pay any rent?"

"Well no... But she might ask for some."

"You'll need to come back to us to update your details when that happens."

"Great... What about a council house?"

"Have you already applied?"

"Yes, weeks ago. In fact about three weeks before I left the army. I'm still waiting for an answer."

"Well, it is rather a long list." As if that was a reasonable answer to why my Indian neighbour had just been given priority over me for a council house.

I thought I would press this aspect further.

"Look, I've just spent almost twelve years in the service of my country. The least that I could be offered is a place to live with my family."

"You've presently got a place to live and anyway, you left the army voluntarily. It is, therefore, of your own doing that you find yourself homeless. That's why your benefits have been limited."

I could NOT believe what I was hearing!

"Nine pounds and forty-five pence a week in return for twelve years of service, and some guy who's been in this country for just three days gets eighty pounds per week. It's a bit unfair, don't you think?"

"I'm sorry you feel that way, Mr Pollard, but they're the rules. I'm afraid I can't do anything about it."

Jobsworth prat!

"I wonder if I would have received more consideration from the guy who authorised the Indian chap eighty pounds per week? I'm sure he would have been more sympathetic than you... "

No answer, no response from the interviewer. He just tapped his papers on the desk and shouted "next!" as if I was invisible.

With that I gathered up my own paperwork and departed from the building, picking up and throwing in the bin the long strip of unused tickets pulled from the soap dispenser's arse.

I even had to wait for several weeks before I received my measly nine pounds and forty-five pence. I made several enquiries with the Labour Exchange about the delay but the excuses were numerous, ranging from "we'll look into it" to "the manager is on his lunch break" to "you made yourself redundant."

My grown-up rogue gene must have wet his pants laughing at me.

CHAPTER NINE

Bill's First Ever Job Interview

WARNING!

From this point onwards my dialogue may damage your health. Particularly your brain because the subject of employment is boring. Crushingly boring.

That's because employment is supposed to be serious. You're not supposed to have fun. You don't get paid to have fun at work. You're paid to be productive and to communicate clearly and to write your reports for the boss and to look smart wearing a suit and tie and clean shoes. So there's not a lot to write about and I'll have to give you some technical stuff occasionally to plump out the pages, to make it look like there's a lot to pique your interest.

Publishers like lots of pages. Lots of pages give the Editor something else to read other than the Beano or this month's car magazine, and lots of pages keep them busy and stops them from playing games on their computers.

Now, I'm not saying there weren't any laughs. I'm sure you'll find some gems hidden in the text somewhere. It's just that I had fewer laughs in employment than when I was in the army. Without my army pals to provide some entertainment I was entirely on my own, and when you're on your own in civvy street entertainment opportunities are few and far between.

However, having made this warning there are a few unusual situations I've found myself in that are worthy of a few lines.

If the dialogue in any of the following chapters gets too boring for you don't do anything stupid like throwing this book, or even yourself, out of the window. Just skip to the next chapter.

***

December 1977

I came to realise that civvy street turned out to be mostly straight laced and serious. I guess that's what should be expected. Nonetheless, lack of opportunity didn't stop my grown-up rogue gene from creating some entertainment of its own.

I started to integrate with my civvy community and I had been to the Labour Exchange to see if there were any draftsman jobs. No chance. Too specialized.

My mother-in-law had moved into the second bedroom of her home to make room for my family and me. We were a bit cramped but at least we weren't homeless. I focussed on my job search, scrutinising local papers and high street employment agencies for jobs in technical drawing. I wasn't having much luck and I was beginning to think that perhaps I'd narrowed the goal posts too much on my choice of employment.

I was also beginning to feel guilty about not being able to provide for my family. Nine pounds and forty-five pence per week didn't go very far. Inflation was rising fast and wages were not keeping up. I was thinking that I would have to take on any job to be able to contribute towards our upkeep. Even sweeping the streets!

Now don't go getting excited about that last statement.

I know that you are thinking "It's not politically correct," or

"What's wrong with sweeping the streets?" or

"It's an important job, keeping the environment clean," and right now, in 2022, I entirely agree. Honestly.

But even before I joined the army the job of sweeping the streets was considered to be the bottom of the barrel with regard to job prospects. The phrase was a 'Sheffieldism'. If you lost your job you never told anybody you lost your job. If someone asked what you did for a living you told them you were 'sweeping the streets' because your self-respect didn't allow you to admit that you were jobless.

Anyway, suffice to say that I was feeling guilty for not being the breadwinner in my family. I wondered if my unsuccessful job search and resultant guilt was being influenced by my grown-up rogue gene.

My wife had a job in the city and Mum-in-law was extremely supportive, but my self-respect and pride wasn't alleviating my guilt. I was beginning to feel useless. Then my luck changed. Grown-up rogue gene must have been asleep, or on holiday, or not paying attention. It obviously took its eye off the ball.

My wife and mum-in-law were staunch Methodists. My wife still is. Although I considered myself to be a Methodist, 'cos that's what my own mum had told me I was, I didn't attend church regularly. However, Mum-in-law was in a conversation with a bloke at the church one Sunday morning and he politely asked about my wife and me. "Were we settling down to civvy life Okay?", "How were the kids?", "Did I have a job?" You know, that kind of small talk. Mum-in-law mentioned that I was looking for work as a draftsman but wasn't having much luck.

You know what? This guy was a Partner in a structural engineering office. He gave Mum-in-law a business card and suggested that I contact him at his office.

On returning home Mum-in-law collared me and handed over the business card with a suggestion that I phone the guy. Now I knew nothing about this bloke, his office or structural engineering but Mum-in-law assured me that he was kosher and that he might know somebody who could give me a job. With a great deal of trepidation I telephoned the number on the card and asked to speak to the guy. He wasn't available at that precise moment but according to the lady on the phone I "could make an appointment to visit him at his office."

I did that 'cos I didn't have anything else to do and I brought Mum-in-law up to speed on events.

"You'd better get a shave before you go," she advised.

A shave? I didn't even have a suit! I did, however, have a jacket and trousers and a tie and I hoped that that attire would be okay. If I needed a suit I would, no doubt, be told and I would have to go get an off-the-peg two piece.

On the day of the arranged meeting I approached the receptionist's desk and volunteered my name. After checking her diary she asked me to take a seat while she notified the boss that I had arrived. He came to meet me.

Warmly shaking my hand he advised that he was unable to speak at length with me, but his Partner was looking forward to asking some questions. I followed him into the Partners' office and took the hand of the other half of the partnership, a friendly guy who smiled broadly and offered me a seat opposite him.

He asked all the questions I was expecting, although I suspect he already knew the answers.

"So, you've just left the army. How are you settling into civvy life?"

"Okay, I think. It's certainly different to what I've been used to."

"Yes, it must be. I hear you are looking for a job as a draftsman. What experience do you have?"

"None. I'm reading a book on geometric drawing and I'm trying to refresh my memory from my school days."

"Oh? Why do you want to be a draftsman?"

The discussion between us followed these lines and lasted for what I thought was ages. I was beginning to get a little nervous. Then the guy sat back and told me how impressed he was with me.

"When do you think you can start work with us?" he asked.

I couldn't believe my ears. I opened my mouth to speak but just could not get my tongue and vocals working.

"I... I... "

"That's okay. I don't need an answer right now. I'll have a word with {Partner} and I'll get back to you shortly. Would you like to have a look round?"

"Yes, please, and thank you for your time."

I shook his hand vigorously and probably squeezed too hard in my enthusiasm.

"Whoa!" he grimaced. "You'll need to be a little more delicate with a drawing pen," he joked.

He telephoned someone in the office and a chap came in to be introduced to me. After a tour round the office I left, thinking "Maybe my grown up rogue gene had decided to quit, at long last."

Wrong...!

So, I now had a job and, importantly, a regular income. The money wasn't great, but it would supplement my wife's salary and it was a boost up for our optimism. The Labour Exchange can stuff their derisory nine pounds and forty-five pence... Somewhere. Not that I'd had any financial help from them since I had requested it. It's now been over a month without any benefit payment whatsoever.

My grown-up rogue gene was now miffed at me for getting a job before he could intervene.

CHAPTER TEN

Bill's First Mortgage

Having secured a job I settled down to my new routine and I could now concentrate on making life for my family a little more comfortable.

We applied for a credit card from our bank. It was called an 'Access Card'... a new way to pay for goods bought over the counter. Anyone remember them?

We had applied for one of these when I was in the army but the bank declined us this facility because we were in the army. At that time army families with a pay grade below the rank of Officer had a bad reputation for repaying the amount spent on credit cards. Officers couldn't default on repayments because they were allowed to take out a loan to repay their credit card debts, something else the rest of us were not trusted to manage. I sometimes wonder just how many Officers 'managed' their credit cards responsibly...

Talking of Officer privileges, I bet you didn't know that when I was in the army only Officers in married quarters were issued with a jelly mould. The rest of the lowly occupants in married quarters didn't get one. Perhaps the army assumed that only Officers' wives were capable of making a jelly? Mind you, looking back at some of the blokes' wives I recollect that that assumption may well have been correct!

However, for a second time we were declined a credit card. This time because I didn't earn enough. The bank never considered my wife's earnings... Grown-up rogue gene's influence once more?

Next milestone? Get a roof of our own for my family.

Now that we had two wages coming in, my wife and I could regularly afford to put a few of pounds away to save for a deposit for a house somewhere local. Had to be local, 'cos we were relying on dear old Mum-in-law to manage the kids while we were at work. One had started primary school and the other was patrolling Mum-in-law's home, emptying the pans and crockery out of cupboards, generally making a mess with paint, chalk, crayons and food, and sneezing snot all over the carpets!

I've never seen so much snot come out of such a small orifice. I've read, on the internet, that humans produce as much as 1-2 quarts of snot each day. It's true. I reckon that my young daughter must have used up all our quotas in just one morning!

Anyway, we started saving as much as we could afford, allowing for our share of household maintenance to Mum-in-law. But we never counted on grown-up rogue gene giving us a helping hand... in the opposite direction!

We found ourselves in the deposit catchup trap.

At that time Building Societies required a deposit equal to ten per cent of the purchase cost of the property one was looking to buy. As time rolled on four uncontrollable events conspired to make house buying extremely difficult:

1. The Building Societies increased their lending rate from six per cent in 1977 to seventeen per cent when we were trying to secure a mortgage in 1980.
2. Inflation rose to a crippling twenty-one point eight per cent.
3. Because of the high inflation rate house prices spiralled out of all proportion.
4. Salary rises were minimal.

The combined effects of these four events made it impossible for us to buy a house.

Each time we saved what we thought was enough to ask for a mortgage, Building Society interest rates had increased, inflation had risen and house prices had rocketed. We were in a perpetual catch-up mode and so could never save enough for a deposit that would satisfy any Building Society's criteria for a mortgage.

I used a lot of my lunch hours and weekends searching for affordable houses and affordable mortgages, all to no avail. There were several potential houses on the market, but from the Building Societies' perspective we didn't have enough deposit or I didn't earn enough.

After three years of saving we never had enough for a deposit. A re-think of strategies was required.

Nanny... That's what our kids called Mum-in-law – Nanny came up with an inspired and innovative idea. I think it was more out of necessity than choice, but they do say that "necessity is the mother of invention."

She, also, had kept an eye on the housing market and she found a single bedroomed flat right next door to the Methodist Church that she and my wife attended. Convenient, eh?

Nanny's suggestion was that we buy her house, the house we were all living in, for the amount that she would need to purchase the flat adjacent to the church.

We talked about it and discussed the pros and cons of this idea. I had to be sure that Nan would be comfortable with the idea and not suggesting it just to find us a place to live. Nan's kindness, however, now meant that the size of a loan in relation to our joint income would satisfy the Building Society's criteria for a mortgage.

We now had enough confidence for my wife and I to apply for a mortgage but there was still one question outstanding. Would we be able to afford the repayments? Only one way to find out.

My wife and I approached a local Building Society with our notes, calculations, proposal and an abundance of optimism. Subject to us finding the deposit the Building Society was more than happy with our plan and agreed to loan the amount requested. The property purchases went through without a hitch and we became owners of a little piece of England, but not without some payback.

Repayment of our mortgage amounted to approximately one thousand pounds per calendar month. Now that's a lot of money in today's terms (2022), but in 1980 that amount was equivalent to a payment of approximately five thousand pounds per month today!

A lot of money, eh? We scrimped and saved for a long time. Several years. No holidays, just an occasional Saturday down at Littlehampton... And we had to sell our car because we couldn't afford to run it.

My wife and I went without the occasional meal but, like my mum and dad, we always made sure the kids were well fed and clothed, and we always tried to give them a Christmas to remember. Back in those days I was frequently struck with a distinct feeling of déjà vu, thinking about my own childhood and what my parents did to keep my family fed, clothed and content with one's lot.

However, having now got a place of our own one thing we could do was rescue our chattels from storage. We didn't have many chattels because the Ministry of Defence had provided everything a married couple needed in their army quarter. Everything, that is, except a jelly mould... Anyway, we had bought our own bedding, some crockery and a settee to make life in the army accommodation more home-like. With the exception of the settee everything we owned had been packed in a few large cardboard packing boxes.

The boxes we didn't need immediately, the boxes full of our sheets, blankets, pillows, pillow cases, towels and spare clothes were stored in the garage at the bottom of the garden. This place wasn't exactly the best place to store stuff because there were copious entry points for all kinds of animals that wanted a place to sleep, but we couldn't afford any commercial storage.

Spoiler alert! Grown-up rogue gene is on the prowl for something to meddle with.

When the time came for me to retrieve our chattels from the garage, I exposed the boxes.

As soon as I touched the one on top it collapsed, spilling a load of chewed-up cloth on the garage floor. Absolutely everything in that particular box had been ruined by mice that had shredded our clothing, and some of the box, for nesting material.

The box below that one was not in any better condition.

The box on the floor was an even bigger surprise. It's difficult to describe what I found with this box. Although the box, itself, was in a surprisingly good condition the contents filling this box was just one block of chewed up fluff forming a mouse's huge nest. The box was full of the stuff, all neatly packed to the box lids. It must have taken months to create this block of chewed and shredded fluff, but I bet it was the Mayfair of mice nests. It must have been really warm and comfortable inside this palatial condominium. As I rolled the box over to empty its contents on the floor dozens of mice scattered throughout the garage, diving for cover in any accessible cavity or heading towards the garage door.

After exposing the nest I decided to clear out the garage to expose any other nests that squatting mice may have made. I found three, all comprising remnants of my bedding and clothes. The only soft furnishing that had survived my army departure was the settee.

This was one of those times that I cursed my grown-up rogue gene out loud!

Now, there's a moral to this infuriating incident... Never, ever, store your chattels in your garage. Even if you don't have two brass farthings to rub together, find the money to store your possessions in a commercial storage unit. Sell your soul, sell your daughter, sell your wife's body. Even take out a second mortgage but find the cost... Somehow. You will not regret it.

Putting aside any future interference from my grown-up rogue gene, my wife and I eventually made it through to the light at the end of this particular tunnel.

CHAPTER ELEVEN

Bill's Bath House

I had never been attracted to buildings.

Never thought about it. Never had to until now, but learning how buildings were constructed gave me an insight into the beauty of buildings. What stops them from collapsing, the variety of materials used, the ground conditions upon which they are built, why they have problems and what problems were significant.

Courtesy of Friends Of Birley Spa

In fact, I learned that Structural Engineers didn't just have to know about structures they had to have a deep knowledge of geology, arboriculture, physical and mechanical properties of the materials used, the effects of wind, rain, sun and impact, and many other sciences that I had never had the need to learn before now.

There was, however, one particular structure that I will never forget. I need to take you back in time to tell you about this building...

It's 1961 and I'm eleven years old and in the final year of my junior school, Birley Spa Junior School. I was fortunate enough to be introduced to Birley Spa Bath House.

Often described as Sheffield's best kept secret, local legend had it that it was once a Roman Bath. Research, however, has confirmed that it was originally a Victorian bath house. It was fed by Birley Spa, a small stream mentioned in historical texts from the eighteenth century as being famous for its therapeutic attributes, both for bathing and for drinking. The Spa probably gave the school its name.

Once a thriving Victorian community hub, the Second World War forced its closure. Never to open again it fell into disrepair. It was virtually unknown to the folks of my generation but I, personally, knew about it because the lane passing by was one of my favourite routes home from school.

Purely by coincidence I once met a bloke working there. I think he was inspecting it for some reason and in true Yorkshire schoolboy fashion I asked, "wot yer doin' mister?"

He asked if I wanted to look inside.

The answer had to be an enthusiastic, "Yes please!"

The entrance door had been secured by a large padlock. The key to this was hidden under a flat stone. Watching the bloke retrieve the key I inwardly filed its location in my memory, thinking "That might be useful one day... "

Inside the building I was mesmerised by what I saw.

Now, at the age of eleven going on twelve I was beginning to take more than a passing interest in girls. If you haven't read my previous book I'll tell you that the school's dark room, for developing rolls of photographic film, was also a convenient place to explore the developing breasts of girls who were more than willing to allow a sneaky fumble when the light went out.

The Bath House became my private den. It's where I took my stash of biscuits that I'd lifted from the biscuit box in the school's dark room. I didn't tell the boys at school about it because I knew it would become crowded and possibly trashed. What I did do was ask a girl if she would like to come with me to see it.

"Roman Baths?" She asked.
"Yea. Here, in Hackenthorpe."
"You're kidding. We don't have one."
"Yes we do, and you can swim in it. Honest."
"I don't have a swimming costume."
"So? Neither do I," my hands upturned and shrugging my shoulders.
There was a pause while she thought about it, "... Where is it?"
"Ah. It's really close by. I'll show you after school."
"... Okay. See you outside the gate?"
"Yep. See you later."

At four o'clock, when we were all granted our freedom, I skipped to the school gate and waited for about ten minutes. I was just beginning to think that I'd been stood up when the girl ran into view from one of the school buildings.

"Sorry I'm late," she smiled, "I had to queue up to pay for my dinners."

School dinners cost us nine [old] pence (9d) per dinner and we had to pay our class teacher on the first day of the school week.

We both strolled down the hill to the Bath House, arms around each other's waists. Retrieving the key from its secret hide-away I opened the door and waved for the girl to enter.

Inside the building she was as mesmerised as I was on my first visit. We tested the water. It was really cold but that didn't stop us from stripping butt-naked and plunging into the bath!

I went down to the Bath House for a swim with several of the girls from school. There was never any embarrassment about naked swimming. At that age nobody cared about nudity. We were too young to appreciate the allure created by nudity, although the girls never minded my roving hands measuring their bra size. One of the girls even encouraged it, saying, "Daddy does it a lot in our shed...!"

At the time, I was too young to comprehend the enormity of that disclosure.

***

During my many solo visits to the Bath House I studied the structure.

I was fascinated by many things. How did they build the circular bath without it leaking? Where did the water enter the building? How did they heat the water? What did they use? Did they have any plans?

I think this fascination with the Bath House instilled in me a curiosity about structures that stayed with me long after the time I started work as a draftsman.

So, I've now got a job as a structural detailer and I've got a roof over my family's heads.

I've now got to build myself a reputation. Not just any reputation, but a good reputation. So my first task was to learn the art of drafting plans.

The purpose of drawing plans, we all know, is to communicate appropriate information to the constructors to enable them to construct what the designers, and of course their clients, want.

With regard to buildings, the architects design the shape of buildings and the structural engineers make sure they stand up, and stay up during so called 'acts of God' – freak weather, floods, earthquakes and the like. The structural engineer's drawings, therefore, were not so much about the look of the building but more about what was inside the structure. Stuff like the detail of reinforcement inside the physical elements.

Now drawing lines on paper isn't as easy as it first seems. They have to be straight, their lengths have to be accurately drawn, to the closest of millimetres, and they have to be drawn to scale.

When I was a draftsman there was a variety of drafting equipment. Special drawing boards, special T-squares, special set squares, special pens, special ink, special erasers to obliterate one's mistakes drawn in the special ink, pencils, pencil erasers, and don't forget special paper. The finished drawing then had to be printed by a special printer and the end result folded in a special way.

Not so today. With the creation and development of computers, draftsmen can now work from home with nothing more than a keyboard, a mouse, a high definition screen and an internet connection to send one's finished article to the boss for approval.

Anyway, the first thing I had to learn when I started work was how to draw numbers and letters. Drawing is one thing, but labelling the drawing had to be concise and, above all else, legible. Each drawing office had its own style of labelling so I spent hours and hours practicing my firm's style of lettering before I was let loose on a drawing of my own.

After a while I got the hang of the key elements of drawing; line thickness, accuracy, speed and, importantly, cleanliness of my work. I settled down to my new life in the office. At the age of twenty-seven I was the oldest office junior in the world, a reality that my good natured and humorous co-workers often reminded me of, especially when a cup of tea was required! My new career was off to a good start.

Maybe my grown-up rogue gene had decided to retire?

CHAPTER TWELVE

Bill's Cracks

As my drawing competence improved I was given more and more unsupervised projects to complete, although there was always an associate partner or graduate of the firm available to check my work.

One of my more satisfying projects was to draw a site plan. I went down to Brighton with a graduate and was the chain man, holding a staff while the graduate measured heights and distances using a theodolite. After three days we returned to the office to convert reams of data into a scaled plan of the site. Great weather, great job, great fun. The boss remarked what a good job we had done.

I was also given the task of visiting a large derelict three storey hotel to take dimensions of the whole building so that I could convert my sketch plans into readable floor plans for an architect. The building was going to be refurbished and the architect wanted to know what all the walls were constructed of. I took a colleague with me, a newbie to the firm, to help me record the dimensions. Back in the office when my plans were complete the boss, again, commented favourably about my work.

After a couple of years drawing building elements I started to focus on a particular discipline within the structural engineering domain. Subsidence of low rise buildings.

Now, a low-rise building can be simply defined as one which is not tall enough to be classified as high-rise. Having said that there is, apparently, little precise consensus as to what constitutes high rise. A high-rise building is defined variously as a building in which the number of storeys means occupants need to use a lift to reach their destination, or the height is beyond the reach of available fire-fighting equipment, or the height can have a serious impact on evacuation. Typically this is considered to include buildings of more than seven to ten storeys.

So one can surmise that a low rise building is one that is up to seven storeys high. That's stretching the definition of 'low rise' a bit, 'cos I would rather jump from a two storey building than a seven storey building. I suppose the description of 'low rise' can be considered as a relative concept.

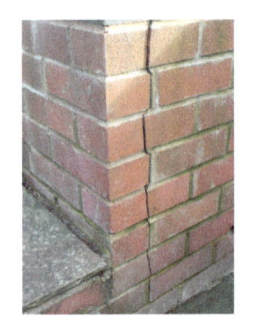

Anyway, my job focussed primarily on domestic properties or, to put that another way, houses. I sometimes had a commercial property to inspect, such as a farm building or a storage unit, but following the long, hot, dry summer of 1976 structural engineers were inundated with instructions to inspect buildings damaged by subsidence.

Subsidence? That can be defined as a reduction in the support of the foundations to a building.

So what happens?

Well, what most people don't know is that the ground on which we build our most valuable personal asset, our homes, continually moves. Now don't go getting paranoid about this and start losing sleep because this movement is so miniscule that it has no effect on buildings, so we never see it happening. But it's there.

Occasionally something influences the nature of the ground on which our foundations have been cast and Insurers have conveniently categorised such influence under various headings; subsidence, heave and landslip. I'm not going to bore you with the technicalities of these events. Suffice to say that many, many buildings have been, and still are, affected by foundation movement.

Okay, back to my progress with the firm.

An associate decided it was time I started to specialise. He took me under his wing and I accompanied him on house inspections. He imparted his knowledge of ground conditions, the reasons for subsidence, the signs to look for, the types of cracks in various wall constructions and the direction of structure rotation, and I absorbed all this information like a sponge. I went round with him, initially recording the dimensions required to draw a working plan while he discussed matters with the home owner. After a while he handed everything over to me, from inspecting the building to interviewing the owner. He became my 'helper', holding the tape while I took dimensions and sitting with me during my discussions with the owner. He always accompanied me on a job and he was always ready to jump in and help me out if I got stuck with a diagnosis or interview.

On return to the office I drew up the plans and designed the underpinning that was required to stabilise the foundations, writing a report to accompany them. At last I had found a niche that I could comfortably develop. I was, to a degree, my own boss although my reports and plans were always vigorously scrutinised before being issued because I wasn't qualified. After all, the firm had a professional liability to protect, as well as their reputation.

Strangely, my rogue gene had not resurfaced for some time.

***

One thing I learned, very quickly, was that home owners were sometimes unpredictable. Very unpredictable.

They were extremely quick to complain about something only they knew had upset them. It doesn't matter what. If you didn't take your shoes off before entering their home they would complain about "mud being walked all over the carpets," despite the fact that there was none. If you took your shoes off they would complain that you had smelly socks, despite the fact that you put a clean pair on every day.

If you said something they didn't want to hear, like, "I'm afraid you've got a little bit of subsidence," they would complain that you were wrong.

In fact, given the opportunity some would find any reason to complain. From, "He didn't finish the cup of tea that I made for him," to "He's got bad breath." Even, "He came casually dressed," noting the absence of a jacket on a day when the temperature was $1000°C$.

I think it's one of Britain's peculiarities. Brits just don't seem to be happy unless they are queuing or complaining... Happy in their own misery.

Ambushes also seem to be an unexpected trait of the British.

I once went to a house with my associate in tow to inspect it for an insurance claim. My external inspection did, indeed, reveal that there had been some foundation movement. A lot actually, probably caused by root encroachment from a large London Plane tree situated about ten yards away on the local authority footpath verge. Cracks had appeared in the usual places, around the window reveals and below the sills on the front and side elevations. Some cracks went up as far as the roof line, indicating a serious foundation problem. I needed to photograph and record all the cracks to enable me to write a detailed report.

The cracks noted outside had probably also appeared in the same locations inside. Mr Homeowner showed us round the ground floor, pointing out the internal cracks.

"Do you want to look upstairs?" he asked.

"Yes, please," I answer, expecting him to show us upstairs.

"Okay. I'm sure you don't need me to show you around. Help yourself," he invited.

"Would you like a cup of tea?" he asked my associate.

"That would be nice, thank you," was the reply.

My associate nodded towards the door, indicating that I should go and get busy upstairs with my camera, tape and clip board. I felt a familiar itch in my ballbag, where my grown-up rogue gene had been reclining...

Off I went upstairs to carry out my inspection.

Bathroom. Done.

Bedroom three, a box room full of... Boxes. Done.

Bedroom one, the master bedroom. What... ? There was a woman in there! She was sat up in bed looking in my direction with a book in her lap and her eyebrows raised in surprise.

"Oh! I'm terribly sorry. I didn't know there was anybody in here," I said, showing some embarrassment. Before she could say anything I reversed out of the room and closed the door. I went downstairs to report that I had inadvertently crashed in on a woman in bed.

"Oh, I'm sorry," Mr Homeowner declared, "I should have mentioned that my wife is not feeling well. Come with me and I'll have a word with her."

We went back upstairs and I entered bedroom two to inspect it while Mr Homeowner briefed his wife. My associate is enjoying his cup of tea downstairs. Mr Homeowner found me writing my notes and drawing my sketch of bedroom two and he tells me it's okay to go into bedroom one now as he has told his wife all about me.

"Thank you," I say, and Mr Homeowner left me to it.

I knocked on the door to bedroom one to make sure Mrs Homeowner is ready for my entrance.

"Come in," I hear, and I gingerly opened the door and entered.

Would you believe it? In the time it had taken her husband to depart from the room and go back downstairs she had removed her nighty and was sat there, half naked and with a finger to her mouth shushing me to be quiet.

I thought to myself, "Just do the job and stay away from the bed."

"Have you come to look at my crack?" she asked, broadly smiling as she pulled some of the bed covers back to expose a leg.

I took a deep breath and puff my cheeks out as I relax my lungs.

"... I've just come to make a few notes," I answer.

I could have answered with something more appropriate but thought better of it.

"Ooo... " she pouted, exposing her other leg.

I ignored the scene in front of me and started to rapidly sketch the walls with my back to her. As long as I can record the location, direction and size of the wall cracks I could hoof it as far as the room dimensions were concerned when it came to drawing this house.

I quickly worked my way around the room and as each minute passed more of the bedcovers got discarded until she laid there, stark naked and laying in a provocative pose.

"Okay," I thought, "Now is the time to make a hasty beeline for the door," but grown-up rogue gene got in the way!

Just as I got to the doorway Mr Homeowner walked in. He looked around and said, "This is cosy, isn't it...?"

"I... I... "

"Are you taking pictures of my wife?"

"No," looking down at the camera in my hand.

"What are you doing with that camera, then?"

"I'm photographing the wall cracks," pointing to the defects. "I need the photos to draw accurate plans."

"How long are you going to be?" hands on hips.

"Er... I've finished," trying to back away from Mrs homeowner who is now wrapping her arms around my waist and squashing her naked breasts against my back.

Mr Homeowner peeled his wife from my frame, my arms outstretched trying not to touch any part of her exposed physique, and I push past him to hurry downstairs.

My associate watched me dash through the hallway and out of the main entrance door with the words "Finished. Let's go," and I showed him my heels as I dashed out of the house and down the garden path to the car.

I must have stood next to the car for maybe ten minutes while I waited for my associate.

He eventually appeared from the house, all smiles, and sat behind the steering wheel. I waited for some words of wisdom, or perhaps an admonishment from him.

I took a breath and was just about to tell my version of events when he interrupted me and said, "It's okay, don't worry. Mr {homeowner} has explained and he has asked me to apologise on his wife's behalf. He should have warned you before you went upstairs. His wife has full-on dementia and she acts that way with anybody who calls to the house. Apparently, she strips off in the lounge, in the kitchen, in the hallway, in fact anywhere there are visitors. Next time anything like that happens come and get me instead of riding it out alone."

Boy! Did I breathe a sigh of relief? When I was upstairs I could see not just my job on the line, but also the reputation and good name of my firm.

Days later one of the Partners phoned down to me to ask if I would see him. I entered his office and he showed me a really nice letter from Mr Homeowner, apologising for his wife's behaviour.

I had to return to the property on several occasions to inspect the remedial works, but I always graciously declined the offer of a cup of tea from either Mr or Mrs Homeowner whenever I was there.

Rogue gene really worked hard to drop me in it that time.

CHAPTER THIRTEEN

Bill Moves On

August 1984

After six and a half years as a draftsman I felt it was time to find a better paid job. The construction industry had stalled and so had salaries, although subsidence jobs kept flowing into the office.

My knowledge of subsidence had greatly improved and I completed my drawings and reports without supervision but with checks to verify accuracy. I had become quite adept at diagnosing, reporting on and supervising repairs for subsidence damage.

Now here's where it gets a bit technical, so feel free to skip to the next chapter if you get bored.

Back in the day, the insurers and their policy holders needed someone to investigate and report on all types of insurance claims. With regard to building damage the insurers' claims handlers needed someone to advise them on its age, severity of damage, the cost of remedial work and, most appropriately, liability... Was the cost of repairing the damage covered by the policy?

There were several types of insurance claims 'advisor'; Loss Adjusters, Loss Assessors, Building Surveyors, Estate Agents and numerous Structural and Civil Engineers. Out of this lot there was only one professional body specifically educated and trained to handle the wide variety of insurance claims that insurers had to deal with... Loss Adjusters.

Loss Adjusters.

These are independent and impartial bodies of professionals appointed by insurers to advise both the policyholder and themselves on all aspects of insurance claims.

Back in those days insurers didn't have anyone with much technical knowledge on the subject of subsidence, so they appointed an appropriate body of trusted technical advisors to get advice.

Most Adjusters dealing with building losses had a background of structural or civil engineering or surveying and so had experience of reporting, advising and supervising repairs and repair costs. That's what made them attractive to insurers. The vast majority of insurers, and Loss Adjusters, regarded loss adjusting as a neutral profession. Neither on the side of the insurer nor the claimant. Their task was to report on the damage and possible costs and to see fair play by all parties involved with a particular claim. Having said that, I can't deny that I have met Adjusters who considered themselves appointed solely to cut costs on the insurers' behalf!

Loss Adjusters fees were normally paid by the insurers.

Structural/Civil Engineers.

Occasionally the policyholder, or sometimes the insurer, appointed a Structural or Civil Engineer direct to progress the claim. This was generally okay with me because the Engineer at least knew what he was talking about.

The vast majority of Engineer type advisors were highly qualified people, accredited by undertaking a lengthy university degree course. After more exams they became members of the Institute of Structural Engineers (IStruct.E) or Institute of Civil Engineers (ICE). Really clever people. However, there were some Engineers that were prejudiced against insurers, so the costs started to creep up once the claim had been accepted!

Engineers' fees were normally paid by the insurers.

Building Surveyors.

These chaps were generally good guys. All the ones I met were professionally qualified and accredited by The Royal Institution of Chartered Surveyors (RICS).

Mostly, they were appointed by the insured direct to report on the damage and remedial works, although occasionally an insurer would appoint a Surveyor to act as Loss Adjuster. The difference here is that a Surveyor is just that... A surveyor, whereas in most cases Loss Adjusters were either qualified Surveyors, qualified structural Engineers or qualified Civil Engineers.

Building Surveyors fees were normally paid by the insurers.

Loss Assessors.

These people were appointed by the claimant (the policyholder) to inspect and report directly to them.

They worked solely on behalf of the claimant and their intention, in my experience, was to get as much money as they could from the insurer, whether the claim was covered by the policy or not.

The cost of proving the claim, the Loss Assessor's fee, was not generally covered by the policy, so the Assessor tried to include their fee as well as the cost of repair within the amount claimed. Assessors' fees varied from ten per cent to thirty per cent of the repair costs which, in the event, could amount to many thousands of pounds. In addition, Assessors would also, again in my experience, claim for stuff that just did not exist. For example, hand printed wallpaper at fifty pounds per drop, or new carpets where none existed. They would even claim for wallpaper when the walls were just flat painted. Anything to inflate the claim.

Having said that I must admit to having met many really fair Assessors, intent on arriving at an amicable agreement on costs for both insured and insurer.

Estate agents.

In my opinion, estate agents knew nothing about subsidence although they mostly did have a qualification in Surveying (Estate Management) that they obtained through exams via the RICS. By having the letters ARICS after their name they considered that they had some credibility.

However, the type of surveying qualification obtained by these so called 'specialists' was, at that time, far removed from the structural knowledge required to diagnose subsidence and handle a complicated claim. As far as these 'advisors' were concerned, if there was a crack there was subsidence but that's not always the case in many occurrences of cracked walls. Most of this type of 'advisor', in my view, fell into the category of Loss Assessor.

Estate agent's fees were usually paid by insurers.

***

Most of my work as a draftsman involved communication with Loss Adjusters so I approached the Director of a firm of Loss Adjusters to see if they had any vacancies. I was taken on as a Building Surveyor.

Working as a Loss Adjuster/Building Surveyor I was mostly based in Guildford. At the time an idiosyncrasy in house construction created a huge deluge of subsidence claims to literally every home insurer – Subsidence of ground bearing floor slabs.

What happened?

Well, I'll try not to bore you with the details. I'll just give you the short version.

From the late 1970s house builders constructed concrete ground floor slabs totally independent of the support offered by the walls. They were ground bearing floor slabs.

Problem was, most of these houses had been constructed in an area where there was a high organic content within the soil. The consequence was that as the organic material degraded (rotted away) the weight of the floors compacted the soil and a gap appeared between the floor and skirting boards. I sometimes measured as much as one inch of downward movement of the floor slab by this cause.

To make matters worse, many of the houses were constructed on sloping sites so the builder had to import lots of hardcore to level up the floors. I've seen floors levelled on as much as 750mm of hardcore at one end. The effect of people walking, children running and teenagers dancing on the floors, and even passing traffic, produced downward movement of the floors caused by vibration and natural consolidation of the infill. Compare this to a well filled bowl of sugar. Lightly tap the bowl and the sugar settles downward. Try it, you'll see what I mean. If the concrete floor is poured onto this infill it will follow the infill's downward movement.

For the floodgates to open it took just one house to be the subject of a failed sale because a building society mortgage inspector had deemed the ground floor(s) to have been affected by subsidence... And it took just one insurer to accept that claim.

Bad news travelled fast.

Neighbours, then friends and family of neighbours, then estate agents, then more mortgage inspectors all got news that if there was a gap between the floor and the skirting, the house was blighted by subsidence, and consequently unsaleable. The media reported on this anomaly with gusto, thereby spreading the fear and panic of ground bearing floor slab subsidence nationally.

Given the nature and degradation of the sub-soil and method of construction it was inevitable that gaps would appear below the skirtings. This inevitability, in my view, put the floor slabs into the category of defective construction specifically omitted from policy cover, but insurers', at the time, took the opposite view and paid out on the vast majority of floor slab claims.

We're not talking about a few properties here. We're talking about whole estates. Hundreds of estates nationwide. I and many other Adjusters were responsible for inspecting and reporting on the ground floor slabs to many, many estates. The area that I covered, personally, was widespread – Surrey and parts of S.W. London, Hampshire, W. Sussex, Kent and Berkshire. There were thousands of properties, all with ground bearing floor slabs, and this was in addition to the other "normal" subsidence claims sent to me by insurers.

The cost of floor slab remedial work, at that time, was not cheap. Per property, fifteen to twenty thousand pounds was spent solely on the building works. On top of that there were alternative accommodation costs, storage of furniture, and fees. The total of the repair cost, back then, equates to approximately fifty to eighty thousand pounds per property at the time of writing (2022).

From the fees generated by this manic activity Loss Adjusting firms got rich, Engineers got rich, Surveyors got rich, Assessors certainly got rich and Estate agents got rich. And the insurers' took a huge hit!

Boy, was I busy! At any given time during my employment as an Adjuster I had in excess of two hundred subsidence claims on my desk. I worked all hours, sometimes a fourteen hour day plus weekends just to keep up with the constant flow of subsidence claims. This was par for the course for many of the Building Surveyors in the loss adjusting fraternity.

Grown-up rogue gene didn't let up at all. Not once. Not even for one minute!

The dry summer of 1976 didn't help, either. This was now generating a high volume of subsidence claims, and to add to our workload the great storm of October 1987 created storm and flood damage claims throughout the south-east of England, with costs for the damage created by this storm valued in excess of two billion pounds by insurers.

The combined effects of these events augmented every Adjuster's outstanding claims numbers by an extra one hundred and fifty to two hundred claims each!

At the time it felt like the whole world was caving in on itself and I was beginning to wonder when (if?) I would see my family again.

CHAPTER FOURTEEN

Bill's Adjustments

Okay, I apologise if I bored you with that last chapter but now that you know what a Loss Adjuster is, and what I was up against. I can go on to recall a couple of ambushes that my grown-up rogue gene had engineered for me.

Ambushes were its favourite pastime, always on the lookout for any situation that could be capsized. Going out and meeting clients face-to-face alone was laden with opportunities for my grown-up rogue gene to create a myriad of hazards to hinder one's employment prospects.

Loss Adjusters had to regard themselves in the same light as a doctor/patient relationship. In the vast majority of claims, the Adjusters' inspections and meetings were with women only, the husbands out earning a crust for their families. Sometimes an Engineer would be in attendance, but most of the time it was just the Adjuster and Mrs Policyholder.

So, for both professional and personal reasons it was completely unthinkable... taboo, to be too personal with the clients. One had to maintain a one hundred per cent professional stance.

A stray look would evoke a complaint of, "He stared at my breasts!"

A smile at the wrong time during a conversation would certainly raise the comment, "He leered at me!"

A misplaced comment, meant in innocent jest, would undoubtedly encourage the most feared complaint ever, "He tried it on with me!"

There were 'hot' phrases that one had to avoid, Such as "Getting up" or "Can I look at it?" or "Can you show it to me?" or "I'll have to see how big they are."

Substitutes like, "Climb up" or "Will you show me?" or "I'll need to measure the crack" were even close to the mark in some cases!

I looked back at the time I was an apprenticed joiner working with a maintenance crew on a multi-storey block of council flats in Sheffield. Working at these apartments I'd been ambushed by frustrated housewives, schoolgirls who wanted to improve their ratings at school, lonely grannies who just wanted to pass the time, prostitutes, druggies who just wanted some cash for their next fix, men dressed in all sorts of weird garments and even women with their daughters to make a threesome. I'd had a good grounding for some of the situations I was faced with during my time as an Adjuster.

At one meeting the lady invited me in and we sat down with a cup of tea while I asked some background questions. Having taken my notes I asked if I could inspect the problem. I would also need to measure the house to calculate if the sum insured was adequate.

"How long will it take? I have to get changed for a lunch appointment," the lady asked.

"Not too long. I'll inspect the internal defects first, then go outside to take the building's external dimensions. Then I'll be on my way."

"Oh... Okay, follow me."

I did exactly as instructed and followed the lady upstairs to the master bedroom. This was where the main defects had appeared.

While writing my notes I heard some rustling behind me. Turning round I saw the lady had stripped her clothes off! She stood there in her bra and pants... And the bra was about to be removed.

Making conversation, she had absolutely no qualms about me being there and appeared to be totally unabashed at her semi-naked appearance. I couldn't believe it. Although I tried to avert my gaze, unsuccessfully may I add, I just knew my grown-up rogue gene was playing games with me.

"I... I...," I stammered.

"Oh dear, I've embarrassed you," she said, smiling and hooking her fresh bra behind her back.

"Er no... Not at all," I replied, trying to look nonchalant and at the same time courteous, but with a deep red face.

"That's okay, then. Help me with my zip?" She asked, having wrestled her dress over her head.

I put my clip board down and eased the lady's zip up her back. She made some comment about my "light touch" but I ignored this, eager to get out of the house.

"I'll just be one more minute," I advised, returning to my clip board.

"No worries," she replied, pushing on her shoes.

Having finished inside the house I concluded my discussion about the claim, bid my farewell and went outside to take the property's dimensions. On the way out to her car the lady enthused about our future meetings to discuss the claim.

"I might need a bit of help with my zip again, after lunch," she smiled.

As attractive as she was, I had to decline her invitation... With some regret, may I add?

It was clear that my grown-up rogue gene had decided to have a laugh.

***

I was once telephoned by an Engineer who suggested it would be appropriate to meet him on site prior to my inspection of a property.

This guy was an Engineer I could trust. A likeable chap who took the trouble to assist with the claim, as opposed to fighting me over the cause and the issue of costs. He usually didn't want to be part of the discussions about the claim between the claimant and myself, but this time he insisted.

Generally, I didn't have a problem meeting 'advisors' on site because they could be useful in discussing the technicalities of the claim with the claimant. Such discussions saved me a lot of time. So I met this guy outside the house.

"I'd better go in there with you this time," he declared.

"Oh?" I give him an enquiring look.

"Honestly, you don't want to go in there on your own!" he warned.

"Why not? Have they got a mad dog or something?"

"Not quite. More like a mad woman."

"What? That's not a nice thing to say about your client," I say, jokingly.

"You'll see."

We went to the door and I knocked. The door was opened by a mature, and rather attractive, woman who invited us into the kitchen. She expressed a little surprise at the Engineer's attendance but he politely answered that it was a normal function of insurance claims. I looked at the Engineer for some explanation but he just sat there impassively while the tea was poured and biscuits were tipped onto a plate.

The Engineer presented me with an accurate plan of the building, with dimensions and the location and size of gaps between the skirting and floor. Another settled floor slab. The plans would save me a lot of time when it came to writing my report, although I was a little surprised because this courtesy wasn't usually afforded to me at such an early juncture.

I finished my discussion and stood up with the Engineer to leave. I was really puzzled as to why the Engineer had insisted on accompanying me. The lady was polite, she was helpful and her discussions were friendly. So what had made the Engineer so cagey about me arriving alone?

Engineer – "Thank you Mrs {insured}. We'll both be in touch."

Me – "Yes, and if you have any queries please don't hesitate to telephone me. I'll do what I can to answer them." I held out my hand in polite withdrawal.

The Engineer had departed from the room while I was being polite.

The lady sidled up to me and thanked me for my help, pressing her body against mine.

"Will you need to come back?" she asked. I began to feel uncomfortable by her closeness, her breasts being deliberately squashed against my ribs.

"Er... Probably," knowing this was probably the wrong answer to give, but thinking about my repair work inspections.

"I'll really look forward to that," she says, her hand sliding down to my crutch.

"I'll write to you when I know the insurer's response to the claim," I say, slowly trying to back out of the door. But she was all over me like a rash by now and it was difficult to prise my way out of her octopus-like arms. She forced one of my hands onto her bottom. As soon as I retrieved this she forced my other hand onto a breast. Retrieve that and my spare hand gets pushed into her crotch! Now I realised why the Engineer was so insistent on having a joint meeting!

Fortunately, the Engineer made an appearance through the door and says, loudly, "We've got a lot of people to see, Mr Pollard!"

With a sigh of displeasure and frustration the lady peeled herself from me and thanked me for my time.

Grown-up rogue gene worked really hard with that one...

It transpires that the Engineer's assistant had had the same welcome as I had just experienced, but it took this guy a hell of a lot more time to extricate himself because he was on his own. He had arrived back at the office dishevelled, shaking like a huge jelly on a train's buffet table and vowing to find another job. One that didn't include meeting a client.

I often wondered how, or if, the builders completed their work without any interruptions.

CHAPTER FIFTEEN

Bill's Tempest

October 1987

I briefly touched on this period in chapter 13, but on the night of fifteenth/sixteenth October a violent extratropical cyclone swept across the UK, the Channel Islands and France. It became known as "The Great Storm."

Hurricane force winds in excess of one hundred and fifteen m.p.h. caused many casualties with damage to land, property and chattels estimated at over one billion pounds. It was later described as a 'one in two hundred year event', the last storm of this magnitude being recorded in 1703. Despite extensive media coverage prior to the event, the severity of the storm took everyone by surprise.

To add insult to injury a BBC weather presenter, on live TV, quashed rumours of a hurricane by reporting to the nation, "... apparently, a woman rang the BBC and said she'd heard there was a hurricane on the way. Well, if you're watching, don't worry... There isn't."

The storm kicked off as a severe depression in the Bay of Biscay and decided to track north-east. The met office forecast, the previous afternoon, predicted 'winds for the Channel and very heavy rain overland,' but nobody could have predicted that just a few hours after this forecast had been broadcast the storm decided to change direction. Severe weather warnings were suddenly issued to emergency responders including the Ministry of Defence and London Fire Brigade. The storm had, by then, become unstoppable.

Gathering intensity it hit the south coast of England in the early hours of sixteenth October. Among the most damaged areas were Greater London, the East Anglian coast, the Home Counties, the west of Brittany, and the Cotentin Peninsula of Normandy.

At Shoreham, in West Sussex, a maximum gust of one hundred and fifteen m.p.h. was recorded, while elsewhere around the south-east area gales of up to ninety-four m.p.h. were recorded. A ship capsized at Dover and a Channel ferry was driven ashore near Folkestone. The highest windspeed in the UK was recorded at Gorleston-on-Sea, with a gust of one hundred and twenty two m.p.h. being registered. The National Grid suffered heavy damage leaving thousands of homes without power, and schools were closed. Because most people used only electric radios (not battery-operated) and TV's there was no effective communication.

Trees were blown down with an estimated loss of these in the region of fifteen million... The town of Seven Oaks became One Oak overnight! Forests, parks, roads, and railways were strewn with fallen trees, many of which were blown onto buildings creating extensive structural damage that, in some cases, rendered a house uninhabitable. Roofs were literally torn from the tops of buildings. Chimney stacks were blown over and crashed into the bedrooms below. Flooding reached heights of up to one metre and many cars, caravans and even whole houses were swept away in the floods.

Twenty-two people were reported to have been killed during the storm, eighteen of which were in the UK.

Throughout the night the noise created by the wind resembled the sound of several trains passing close by. Sleep was not on anybody's agenda.

Predicting that the office from which I worked as a Loss Adjuster would be inundated with storm claims, I washed, dressed and bolted down my breakfast at five-thirty a.m. on the morning of sixteenth October. The wind was still howling, the rain was horizontal and whilst driving down the A3 to Guildford that morning I had to fight my car's steering to keep a straight trajectory.

Leaving a flooded Surbiton underpass and heading into the countryside I noticed that almost the whole length of the A3 was lined with fallen trees. As I charged down the carriageway, being battered by small branches, leaves, stones and heavy rain a large tree materialised to the left of my peripheral vision about one hundred and fifty metres away. It was a whole Oak tree... Root bowl, trunk, branches, the lot! And it was horizontal, floating gracefully about two to three metrer above the ground towards the carriageway. It was as if someone had drawn a portrait picture of a tree and then rotated it to view it in landscape mode. It was a surreal sight. Like a film shown in slow motion.

At sixty-five m.p.h. I had a choice to make; stay on this trajectory and risk bombing into the tree or slam the brakes on and risk being blown into a sideways roll by the hurricane force wind. My immediate thought was "When ya gotta go, ya gotta go" and I chose to shove my accelerator pedal to the floor and pray that I got to the tree's crossing point before the tree.

I didn't make it!

Good fortune, however, smiled on me that morning. For some reason the horizontal tree stalled over the carriageway and maintained a height of about three metres. I converged with it at a point almost in the centre of its trunk and the aerial attached to my front wing scraped against the tree trunk as I raced underneath. Lucky, or what?

Breathing a huge sigh of relief I looked in my rear view mirror to see the tree inelegantly plummet to the ground immediately behind me. With an abundance of relief I burst into uncontrolled loud laughter. Maybe my rogue gene had taken its eye off the ball by hiding from the storm...

At eight forty-five a.m. the phones in the office began to ring. They rang incessantly throughout the day and during working hours for the next two to three months. Weekends off didn't feature in the frenzy of claims that had to be investigated.

Ultimately, the storm cost the insurance industry a sum in excess of two billion pounds.

Shortly after the storm abated a colleague and I were seconded to the firm's Brighton Office for three weeks to help out with their storm claims, not that we didn't have enough on our plates with our own Guildford claims. We had to manage these at the same time!

***

While we were in Brighton my colleague managed to cleverly side-step his rogue gene with a bit of lateral thinking.

Similar to many resorts around the UK, Brighton had a row of about two hundred beach huts lined up on the sea front hardstanding between the town and the beach. The storm had swept these into the sea. It was quite a sight watching all those beach huts bobbing up and down in the waves a couple of hundred metres out at sea, heading for the Atlantic Ocean with the outgoing tide. My mate got a 'class action' claim for all of them from various underwriters.

In today's terms a single beach hut costs, on average, thirty-six thousand pounds to purchase outright. To rent one for a month costs approximately two thousand one hundred and fifty pounds. A lot of money, eh? Back in the day those costs would equate to approximately eleven thousand seven hundred pounds and seven hundred pounds respectively. Still quite a wedge even back then and with loss of rental earnings writing off all those beach huts as total losses would have been a huge outlay for insurers. My mate had to think, and work, quickly if he was to save the insurers' from such a big hit. He got his brain into top gear...

He hired a local fishing boat for the day for a few hundred pounds, the amount a fishing vessel would have earned for a day's haul in fish. He then instructed the boat owner to go out and tow every one of those beach huts back to Brighton. Like a comic caterpillar the beach huts were tied together and towed back. For another couple of hundred quid a crane was hired and every one of those beach huts were re-seated in their proper place on the hardstanding.

The hut owners and insurers' were well pleased and my mate was awarded many house points for his lateral thinking.

Loss adjusting was like that – finding ways to resolve a claim to everyone's satisfaction.

CHAPTER SIXTEEN

Bill's Close Calls in a Smart Suit

The great storm of October '87 created a deluge of claims for damage to all types of structures.

Late one afternoon I was telephoned by one of my Directors with a request to go to Ramsgate Harbour to report on a collapsed sea wall. I took a colleague with me to help with my inspection. A building Surveyor I'll call 'M'.

We arrived early evening and located the port's management hut. A guy there showed us where the sea wall had been damaged by the massive waves crashing over it during the storm.

Okay, perhaps now is the time to explain the nature of construction of this wall, and why it collapsed. You'll need to know this in a minute.

If you Internet search Ramsgate you'll see that the Port of Ramsgate has been constructed on a large area of land reclaimed from the sea. To reclaim this land huge car sized boulders were imported from somewhere that didn't need them and stacked on the seabed in a long line to form the outer wall of the reclaimed area. This line of boulders was maybe twenty to twenty-five metres high and about five to six metres wide. Now, with all that mass you would think that absolutely nothing would shift the wall, but the storm proved to the contrary.

The voids within the inside face of the wall were filled with pocket-sized aggregate and hardcore and a scrim coat of chalk was smoothed over this. Heavy duty plastic sheeting was then placed against the scrim-coated inner face of the wall to prevent leaching out of the material tipped into the area between this and the existing land mass.

The area was then filled with a mixture of hardcore to add bulk, together with highly compacted chalk to fill the voids created by the hardcore. A concrete topping was then poured over the chalk to provide a hardstanding.

There you have it. An area of land reclaimed from the sea.

Along came the storm and with it huge waves that towered over the wall and crashed down onto the hardstanding.

Prolonged crashing of waves onto the hard standing set up a chain reaction that became irreversible.

The hardstanding fractured, allowing water to penetrate the infill. At the same time the suction created by the receding waves forced the boulders to move, tearing the inner lining.

With a deluge of water entering the infill from the top, combining with the suction of the receding waves, chalk infill was quickly washed through the torn lining. The sheer volume of water accumulated behind the wall added to the effects of wave suction and sections of the wall collapsed, spilling the infill onto the beach below.

'M' and I began our survey of the damage. It was now beginning to get dark and I wanted to get some decent photographs of the damage for my report to the insurers. Specifically the torn lining. 'M' was down on the beach about twenty or thirty metres to my right as I gingerly eased my way down the side of a boulder on the hardstanding side of the wall. My shoes began to slide on the slippery surface and as my speed of descent increased I decided that it may be more appropriate to stand on a chalky outcrop about two metres from the boulder.

Grown-up rogue gene decided it was time to take over!

Making a jump to the chalky outcrop I landed with a splash as the ground gave way beneath my feet and I abruptly sank into the chalk infill. I was more worried about my camera than I was about my smart suit and I put the camera on top of a nearby lump of hardstanding.

To my horror I suddenly realised that I was continuing to sink into the chalk. Really fast. I was up to my knees in no time!

Uttering profanities about my suit trousers being ruined and giving my grown-up rogue gene a few choice names I struggled to free myself from the chalky quicksand, but the suction of water from this just increased my rate of descent. Now past my knees I thought I had better get some help.

"M?" I called. No response.

I tried again. "M?" Still no response. I'm still sinking.

"M?" a bit louder. This time I got a distant "Yea?"

"Can you come 'ere? I need some help."

"Hang on a minute."

"M, I really need you to help me," panic creeping into my voice. I'm now up to my waist and still disappearing into the chalk.

"Hang on! I'm in the middle of something." If only he knew what I was in the middle of!

"M, I need you, right now!"

"Oh, all right," a frustrated answer. I'm now up to my belly button!

I pleaded, "M. I'm in trouble here and I need you... like yesterday! HELP ME!"

'M' took the hint and I heard him muttering some unprintable words as he climbed up the remnants of the boulder wall. I'm now up to my chest. I decided that if I was going to sink below my headline someone will want something to pull me out... Eventually, so I held my arms straight up. You know, like when you are on a roller coaster and screaming.

'M' appeared and gasped in surprise. "Wait there," he ordered, as if I was in any position to go anywhere else. To my horror he took off.

Cursing profanities at him for leaving me I thought he had bottled it and run away in fright. But he returned after a few minutes with the guy from the management hut. I was now up to my armpits.

The guy threw the end of a rope to me. Grabbing hold I reached out to retrieve my camera. For some strange reason I was still worried about losing it.

"Catch," I shout to 'M', throwing my camera in his direction.

The guy instructed me to loop the rope round my chest three times and tie it off with a granny knot. He dashed off and a few seconds later I heard a diesel engine fire up.

"Hang on" shouted 'M' and suddenly the rope leapt out of the chalk as the slack was taken up by the reversing of a JCB attached to the other end. To my relief I was slowly pulled from the mire. I stood on the pavement, looking like a tube of toothpaste and I asked, "Is my camera Okay?"

My left shoe had been sucked from my foot and was now encased in perpetuity in the chalk. In a few thousand years time that'll be found by some futuristic person in a tight fitting plastic suit and it will be given prime spot in a museum of antiquities. I'm sure there will be lots of learned discussion about what it was, how old it was and what function it served. I bet they will think it was something to drink out of...

"Your camera?" questioned 'M'. "Is that all you were worried about?"

"Well, I'd be more than annoyed if I'd left this place without any photos... "

The management guy went off to fetch his boss.

I couldn't go home in such a mess so I decided that the only thing to do was wash the chalk from my clothes. There was no better place than down on the beach, sitting in the surf.

The look on the boss's face was a picture when he arrived to see me sat there, wallowing in the surf at nine o'clock in the evening surrounded by a milky white patch of chalky water.

***

I didn't enjoy handling storm claims.

There were too many and there was always a golden opportunity for the policyholder to make a killing at insurers' expense.

One of the problems, I found, was that because of the vast volume of claims submitted to insurers they had to deal with some themselves. They never asked any questions about the damage and merely paid out without any checks on the veracity of the claim or, indeed, the costs.

In doing so they made a rod for their own backs. They became 'fair game' for many fraudsters. This set a huge precedent that invited lots of media attention and as soon as Adjusters started to ask questions about the costs, while they were handling a claim, the claimant would shout "FOUL!" forcing his insurer to cave in and pay what was demanded.

I've seen complete new roofs replacing old, decrepit structures that should have been demolished many years prior to submission of the claim.

I've had many 'discussions' with insurers about the folly of totally re-tiling a roof with just a couple of tiles missing.

This philosophy put all Adjusters between a rock and a hard place. If they didn't recommend settlement because the claim was 'iffy' a complaint was made and the insurer paid up. If, however, the Adjuster 'rubber stamped' the claim the insurer got uppity and asked why. I've even had to deal with complaints from the claimants themselves, alleging that I had paid a claim when I should not have.

I began to recognise that Adjusters were in a no-win situation. Especially with grown-up rogue genes like mine!

On one particular occasion I went to a home in the St George's Hill estate, an up-market gated private community in Weybridge, Surrey. At the time, the estate had golf and tennis clubs and was home to many famous TV, film and pop celebrities.

I was invited into the house by a celebrity's wife, offered a cup of tea and a plate of biscuits and shown a damp patch with mould growth in the bathroom. Returning to the kitchen the lady was adamant that the mould "wasn't there before the storm."

I decided to make a closer inspection on my own to see if there was any movement in the window frame, a possible indication of storm damage. There was none. Clearly, the mould patch had appeared because there was no ventilation in the bathroom, and mould spores just love a warm, dark, damp wall on which to proliferate.

On the way out of the bathroom I almost bumped into the maid who was waiting for me to appear.

"That mould has been on there for weeks," she whispered. "I keep cleaning it off, but it just comes back again. I think she...," pointing downstairs, "just wants her bathroom re-decorated."

I had already perceived this the first time I saw the mould patch. I just wanted to make sure with a closer inspection. The maid quietly disappeared back into the bedroom where she was making the bed.

The lady of the house appeared from the stairway. In the bathroom doorway I recommended that she installed an extractor fan and opened the window occasionally to provide some ventilation.

"Was the mould patch covered by insurance?" she asked.

"I'm afraid not. I'll put it to insurers and see what they say but it's doubtful they will accept the claim because mould growth is specifically excluded from the policy." I pointed out the appropriate clause in the policy document she had provided.

The lady then took me completely by surprise. "I'll do anything to have the claim accepted," she declared, at the same time undoing the buttons of her blouse and exposing her bra. I repeated what I'd already told her but that didn't make any difference. With all the buttons on her blouse undone she unfastened the front of her bra to expose her exquisite figure.

Smiling and taking hold of my hand she gently squashed it against one of her exposed breasts.

Blushing profusely, and with some regret may I add, I gently peeled my hand from the woman's breast, apologised and made my exit as politely and quickly as I possibly could. I didn't mention the lady's offer to me in my report. In fact, I've never mentioned it to anybody... Until now.

A couple of weeks later I was instructed by the insurer to close my file. They had 'negotiated' a settlement with the lady despite my report that the defect was not covered. The insurer was apologetic but declared that they did not want any adverse publicity from such a famous client's wife. It seemed that fame had many advantages.

Grown-up rogue gene had struck again.

With situations like that my cynicism increased and I decided that it was, perhaps, time to re-think my employment status.

A cynical Loss Adjuster is not a good Loss Adjuster.

CHAPTER SEVENTEEN

Bill's Many Frustrations

During my time as a Loss Adjuster my negotiating skills improved and I thought it would be a good idea to become a qualified Arbitrator.

So I attended night school in London and passed the examination to attain the title of Associate of The Chartered Institute of Arbitrators (ACIArb). I could now have some letters after my name on my business cards, a badge that would provide some credibility to my existence. Twelve months later I passed the exams for the title of Member (MCIArb).

In addition to that I was also invited to submit my CV to the Association of Building Engineers. I was approved as an Associate Building Engineer (ABEng). Another badge.

I was also asked, by a leading insurer, to re-write the wording of their subsidence policy.

My version was approved by one of my firm's Directors as well as the insurer. This re-write was sent to the insurer's overseas head office for endorsement and re-printing of their policy. Badge number three.

In the midst of all this I had articles on claims handling published by two respected professional journals; one published for the insurance industry and the other for the Institute of Structural Engineers. Badge four.

On top of all this, in 1986 my wife and I had accrued enough savings to apply for a mortgage for a larger home.

I was beginning to be proud of my achievements since leaving the army. Not bad for a lowly trombone playing labourer's son from Sheffield, but on several occasions I was viciously attacked by my grown-up rogue gene.

I was frequently reminded about the old adage that 'pride comes before a fall.'

***

September 1986

The first of several disappointments came as I was in the process of negotiating with estate agents for a new home. My wife and I had seen one advertised that suited our requirements. We were shown round by the owner and we agreed a price there and then. Shaking hands on the deal we departed from site and immediately went to our building society to arrange a suitable mortgage. We had saved a substantial sum for the deposit and we were approved almost immediately.

Next was the business of selling our current home.

Spoiler alert! My grown-up rogue gene had 'got the huff' about my success and decided to upset things.

Although we were ready to purchase our new home we were in the usual house buying queue, waiting for the purchaser of our current property to arrange his own mortgage.

Having had a couple of tentative enquiries for the purchase of our current home I set up a meeting with our new home owners to explain the situation, stressing that even if our present purchaser opted out of the purchase we had enquirer number two on the hook as a standby.

The owners were pretty laid back and agreed to wait before they arranged their move to give us time to sell our present abode. Really nice people, I thought.

Our purchaser number one did, indeed, back out because he was unable to get a mortgage so we immediately notified our enquirer number two who confirmed that he would put steps in hand to purchase our house for a cash sum.

What I didn't count on was the avarice of the estate agent. He had been notified, by our purchaser number one, of his retreat.

Now, the greedy agent had had a number of applicants wanting to view the same property that we had recently struck a deal and shaken hands on. Incredibly, I was notified by the owners of that house that the estate agent had literally kicked us out of the loop by introducing a cash buyer for the house, and this cash offer had been accepted. The owners informed us that the estate agent had told them that my wife and I, we "were no longer in a position to purchase their home because my purchaser had pulled out!"

Despite the fact that we had a cash buyer on the hook we lost the purchase of the house we wanted. I went to the estate agent's office and had a row with him. Water off a duck's back! I should have sued the pants off the guy for misconduct. He had no right to gazump us in the way he did, just to achieve a quick sale for a quick profit.

In the event, we were able to find another home to relocate to and the process of buying and selling was completed without any involvement from that particular leach.

Perhaps I should have asked my grown-up rogue gene for permission to move home?

***

August 1991

I decided to move on from being a Loss Adjuster. The sheer volume of work, coupled with an armful of cynical claims, helped me to come to terms with the fact that I just wasn't enjoying loss adjusting any longer.

I had often asked myself, "Why work your fingers to the bone when you can work just as hard for yourself and reap all the benefits?"

So I made that long leap to self-employment and resigned from my job

Frustration number two coming up, no doubt encouraged by my grown-up rogue gene.

I favoured the idea of working with technology. I bought a desktop PC. A top of the range model with a pair of five and a quarter inch floppy disc drive units. I also purchased a PC database programme that I could adapt, to input information appertaining to subsidence; what, where, when, who repaired and how much.

I set up meetings with the underwriters to the majority of leading insurers to establish the need for this type of database. The responses were phenomenal. Every one of those underwriters agreed that such a database would benefit all insurers, and many agreed to send to me their historic database of claims.

I spent several weeks inputting some data and checking on the reliability of my product and I was ready to go. My marketing letter went out to the insurers inviting them to contact me for information and then guess what? Grown-up rogue gene decided that he didn't want me to succeed.

Out of the blue I received a telephone call from the Association of British Insurers (ABI) effectively squashing my idea by confirming that all insurers had been instructed not to use my database by the ABI. This took me by surprise because all the members of the ABI were, in fact, the very same underwriters that I had met to discuss my proposals... The same ones who had all agreed that it was a good idea!

Because my database never took off I was, once more, unemployed.

Back to the soap dispenser with a stream of tickets hanging from its arse just inside the door of the Labour Exchange.

***

March 1992

After much newspaper and trade magazine searching, along with numerous trips to London to be interviewed by head-hunting employment agencies, I was offered an interview with a firm of insurance brokers based in London City. Old Street to be precise.

I'd never been in this field before but my knowledge of defects in low rise buildings helped me to get the job.

At my job interview I found out that this particular firm of brokers was an in-house company solely owned by an organisation that owned a luxury shipping line. The mother company also owned high end international construction and mining companies and I was given the job of account handler for a mining company that was sub-contracted to dig tunnels and mine coal.

During this period I was also invited to provide lectures to the Institute of Structural Engineers. In partnership with a well-known and well respected Structural Engineer, I provided talks on the insurance aspects of making a claim for subsidence, my lecture partner giving talks on the methods and practicalities of the repairs.

Another badge in my collection of proud moments but once more my grown-up rogue gene stuck his foot out and tripped me up, introducing frustration number three!

Just as I was settling in and looking forward to promotion, the broking firm I worked for was taken over by an international firm of brokers and so, in August 1994, I was made redundant.

It seemed that my grown-up rogue gene, like me, wished we were back in the army.

***

While we're on the subject of commuting to the City, let me digress from employment for a while to tell you about a most surreal incident that took place while I was on my way home one evening.

To get to the office I had to negotiate three different train rides; overland from Worcester Park to Waterloo, change at Waterloo for the Waterloo & City underground line to Bank, and then change at Bank for the Northern Line to Old Street. The journey home was in a reversed path. Not a bad journey once you get used to it, but the commuters on the Northern Line were notoriously packed like sardines into every corner of every carriage. Not one square inch of space was available once the carriage doors eventually closed.

I say 'eventually' because the doors always made several attempts to slide shut before every one of the impatient commuters had squashed their brollies, coats, briefcases, elbows, knees, stomachs and bums away from the inside face of the doors to allow these to fully close.

Each time the doors opened to allow people to clear their obstruction there was always one enterprising guy that saw six inches of space inside the carriage that could be filled. So with a mighty heave he pushed those unfortunate enough to be next to the doors further into the carriage so as to create a couple of extra inches to occupy. He squashed his way into the carriage, like forcing a size nine foot into a size four shoe!

Nobody had any need to hang on to anything during the journey because we were self-packed into a tightly standing throng that couldn't move until the train arrived at a station. The mass of bodies then spilled out onto the platform when the doors opened, like hundreds of marbles escaping from a box that had been tipped onto its side.

Now, there was an unwritten rule of underground rail travel that everyone had to abide by. I learned this rule pretty quickly when I started to commute on the underground.

When you're compacted into a train carriage the rule is that you never... And I mean never, ever, get squashed face-to-face against an unfamiliar person. On the very few occasions I found myself squashed face-to-face with a stranger I soon realised that one could easily be overcome by the smell of last night's beer being breathed into one's nostrils, or the smell of sweaty armpits percolating upwards from shirts and blouses that had been slept in, or wafts of halitosis from badly maintained teeth or the remains of a lunchtime Sushi. I found the smell of second hand Sushi to be the foulest of all.

Another reason not to get locked into a face-to-face squash is women. I've got nothing against women. I love 'em. Every one of them. I'm married to one. But let's face it, there is nothing more embarrassing than being forced to compress against a buxom size 40DD pillow taking up several square feet of valuable standing space. It's okay if it is an intentional squash somewhere private, say, in your office after going home time or in the stationery cupboard or in some non-descript hotel somewhere out of sight, but not on a London underground train.

Nervous smiles all round. And lots of things can happen in that unintentional scenario; a slap on the face, a knee in the crutch, police...

So you make absolutely sure that you get packed into the carriage front-to-back with the person you follow onto the train. Even then stuff happens, no doubt encouraged by everyone's grown-up rogue gene's twisted sense of humour!

I recollect a time when I was innocently stood there, arms securely trapped against my rib cage while waiting for the train to arrive at my station. I suddenly felt my balls being caressed by an unfamiliar hand. I knew this hand wasn't mine 'cos I could feel my fingers trapped against the side of my legs. Nope. Definitely not mine.

I managed to guide my right arm around my torso and lock a vice-like grip onto the unfamiliar fingers. Clamping hard to stop the hand from fleeing I waited until there was enough room to manoeuvre my arm. The hand's owner stared, wide eyed, at my grinning face.

People began to disembark and, with more room to manoeuvre, I twisted the guy's fingers until there was a loud crack as several of his metacarpals parted company from the knuckles of his hand. It was a most satisfying crunch... For me, anyway.

Much to everyone's surprise the guy let out a noisy scream that woke up some sleeping commuters and everyone looked at this guy as if he was deranged.

He disembarked from the carriage trying to cradle his broken hand and with his brief case precariously dangling from the little finger of his other hand. What could he do? Attack me? No chance. Not with only one good hand. Call the police? No way. What would he tell them? That he had just caressed the balls of some bloke who broke his fingers and disappeared into the crowd? Nah!

Anyway, I still haven't imparted my surreal incident to you, have I?

Well, on my way home one evening I decided to pig out on a toffee apple that I bought from one of the station shops at Old Street. Friday, as we all know is 'poet's day', and the tube line was particularly busy with guys like me bunking off early for a weekend of love and laughs and BBQ's and drinking, but not necessarily in that order.

Anyway, here I am with my toffee apple held in front of me with just one bite taken from it. That bite loosened the apple on its stick and I was just trying to position it into my mouth for another bite when the train arrived. Everybody surged forward and I got pushed into the carriage. There was the usual body squash while we disappeared into the tunnel and after a short while the train slowed and entered the next station. My stop.

As I got off the train I was disappointed to find the toffee apple missing from the top of its stick. I thought I had dropped it onto the platform during the push to board the carriage, but as I stepped onto the escalator rumbling up to ground level I looked up, as you do, and saw it.

My toffee apple was now stuck to the back of a woman's coat about six or seven people ahead of me. That coat was definitely going to need dry cleaning but I'm not going to say anything in case I get the blame. So on I travelled to my next underground train, this heading towards Waterloo station.

Would you believe it? After disembarking from this train I saw my toffee apple hitching a lift on some bloke's jacket pocket on the escalator chugging upwards towards Waterloo's main concourse. Yep! Definitely mine. Still with that single bite in it. The apple's exposed flesh is now to turn brown and is looking distinctly dusty so I wouldn't want it returned to me anyway.

At Waterloo I'm waiting for the departures board outside platform eleven to indicate that it was okay to board my train to Worcester Park. I was rudely pushed in the back by some ignoramus rushing to board the train on platform five. I was just about to shout a profanity at this guy when guess what? I saw my toffee apple stuck to the back flap of his jacket. An entirely different guy in an entirely different suit with an entirely different brief case, but with the same toffee apple attached to him. I knew it was mine because I recognised the teeth marks in the single bite that had been taken from it, so I let the guy carry on to his train seat. I'm sure he'll find my toffee apple, but I doubt that he'll be too pleased.

Amazing, eh? Ridiculous but true!

That toffee apple must have been the most travelled toffee apple in England. Three rogue genes had successfully played a game of 'pass the toffee apple' and my own grown-up rogue gene had surely instigated this game to amuse himself. My fellow passengers on the train home to Worcester Park must have thought I was an imbecile, chuckling to myself...

Anyway, back to my discourse about my employment frustrations.

Where was I? Oh, yes. I was in the middle of telling you about my redundancy from a firm of insurance brokers.

***

August 1994

I was kept on by the new owners of the broking firm as part of a team of ten employees to close the firm down and ensure a smooth handover. Apart from this team, and a couple of guys absorbed by the mother company, everyone else accepted a generous redundancy package and dispersed to find another job.

A team of employment specialists from the mother company's Human Resource department came to the office during our shut down to interview the remains of the broker firm's employees and to help find them another job.

I was asked if I wished to attend an interview for a job as the technical advisor to an insurer based in Croydon. Having worked with insurers in the past I was a little hesitant to be one of a much disliked profession. I thought, however, that the invitation to be interviewed was a bit of good fortune because it was, at least, a job to help pay the mortgage, and the trip to Croydon was infinitely better than the haul to London City.

Unbeknown to me, at the time, my grown-up rogue gene was setting me up for another fall. Frustration number four was peering over the parapet.

Having accepted the job in Croydon, I suddenly found that my redundancy pay was cancelled on the basis that I would not suffer any hardship by relocating from one job to another. Other employees had been paid hundreds of pounds, but I couldn't complain because I at least had a job to go to. Mind you, I was a bit miffed that some of those made redundant were re-employed by the takeover company a few weeks later.

My new employer was relocating from shared offices elsewhere in Croydon to occupy a new build office block adjacent to Croydon rail station. I was taken on as their Technical Advisor.

Despite my expertise with buildings' losses my first job with this insurer was to deal with motor claims. I had never been involved with motor claims, except when I made a claim myself, so I knew nothing about dealing with motor claims from an insurer's perspective but that mattered not to the claims manager. However, word got round that I was available to answer technical queries on buildings losses and the staff started to approach my desk.

Guess what? The firm decided to relocate to Northampton and I had no alternative but to accept redundancy once more. I didn't want to relocate my family to Northampton, but grown-up rogue gene clearly knew that, didn't he? It's just as well, really, 'cos I couldn't honestly see a future for me in insurance. As a final insult to injury, I couldn't claim any redundancy payment because I had not worked long enough at the company.

For a fourth time my disappointment made me wonder when… If my grown-up rogue gene would give me a break.

Not for a while, though.

CHAPTER EIGHTEEN

Bill's Advanced Education

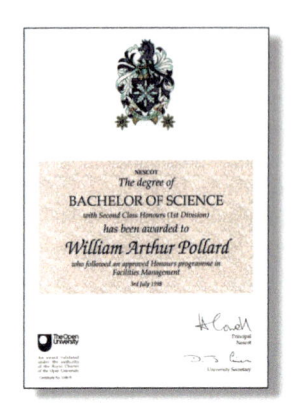

January 1996

In my younger days one of my favourite weekend pastimes was to watch the science programmes on TV. Sunday afternoons were the best times to get horizontal on the settee, switch over to BBC 2 and watch all kinds of interesting science discussions, presentations and experiments.

Because I left school when I was fifteen years old, I never sat for O levels or GCSE's. I didn't, at that stage, want to. But in later years I kicked myself for not staying on to sit those exams and throughout my working life in civvy street I came to appreciate the importance of those bits of paper... Certificates. Something to wave in front of employers.

In almost every job I've done I continually got the same old comment thrown in my face.

"You're doing a fantastic job, but you don't have any qualifications so we can't promote you to office manager," or "supervisor" or "team leader."

Even when the manager retired or died or got the sack the boss would say to me, "Can you manage the office for a while until we employ someone more qualified?"

That took the biscuit. It's tantamount to saying to me, "You're capable of running this office but you won't get a manager's salary and you won't be able to use the title of manager or use his office, and when we do find someone more qualified, you will have to revert to walking around on the bottom of someone's shoe."

So, when I became unemployed, once more, I started the long haul of trawling newspaper & magazines and attending the Labour Exchange in the hopes that I would find a job that I could settle down to and enjoy. After all, I was a mere forty-six years old, with nineteen more years of work left in me.

Then a surprising thing happened and grown-up rogue gene was taken completely by surprise.

My daughter asked me to accompany her to a local college open day to see if there was any course available that would appeal to her sense of adventure. This particular college was affiliated to the University of Surrey.

Browsing the many stands and counters displaying potential courses she saw something that interested her and off she went to ask some questions, leaving me to stand around like a spare part.

A suit inside a gown sauntered up to me and asked if I needed any help. Pointing my daughter out I explained that I was here in the position of taxi driver, and we got chatting.

This chap was the head of the Facilities Management course and after explaining what facilities management entails he went on to tell me that he had a couple of places available.

Now this interested me. Facilities Management is a science. If you Google Facilities Management you'll be given a long winded description along the lines of 'Facilities Management (FM) is a profession that encompasses multiple disciplines to ensure functionality, comfort, safety and efficiency of the built environment by integrating people, place, process and technology.' You can condense this by saying 'It is the science of managing a building and everything inside, except the people.'

Discussing my employment history, and the fact that I was currently unemployed, this guy informed me that I had all the attributes of a Facilities Manager; building construction and repair, insurance, negotiation, financial acumen and, importantly, leadership qualities.

"Come and talk to me" he suggested, thrusting a business card into my top pocket.

I thought about his comments and, having discussed what I saw and heard at the college open day with my wife, I decided to give the guy a call.

A more formal interview was arranged and after making copious notes the guy offered me a place on his full time degree course as a mature student, starting in February 1996.

Ironically, my daughter didn't find anything to her liking.

At forty-six years old I must have been the oldest student in Surrey, and whenever we went abroad for a holiday I always got some extra scrutiny by the chap in the immigration booth inspecting my passport and entry papers asking what my employment was.

I was regarded as a bit of a novelty at college. There was always plenty of light hearted banter in the refectory.

"Let me carry your tray for you dad," or

"Sit yourself down old man while I get your sandwich," or

"Someone fetch a Zimmer frame for this bloke," but I always gave back as good as I got and I was always welcomed to any table.

I enjoyed college life for the next two and a half years. It was bloody hard work at my age though. I had to compete with eighteen year olds who had just left school and learning was fresh in their brain cells. Not only did I have to catch up on all the work I should have done, had I taken GCSE's, I also had to learn all the new stuff for the degree.

In June 1998 I went to college for the last time to get the results of my exams. It was a huge relief to find that I had been awarded a 2:1 degree, with honours, by the Open University.

I was now a Bachelor of Science in the field of Facilities Management. Another badge for my future business cards.

Maybe, from now on, I can find a job and not be told that I am unqualified.

CHAPTER NINETEEN

Bill's Return To The Treadmill

You might be asking why I slipped that last chapter into my section on employment.

Well, gaining a degree certainly pushed me up a couple of rungs on the desirable employee ladder.

It was time for me to return to work. My wife had supported me while I was at college but my pride wouldn't allow me to be a 'kept man' any longer.

Once more I started my newspaper searches, but to my surprise I received a telephone call from someone who was looking for a Facilities Manager and had been given my name. I had absolutely no idea how this guy got my name and phone number but I eagerly agreed to an interview, although the venue for this interview turned out to be even more surprising. We agreed to meet at my local pub!

I wondered if grown-up rogue gene was up to something sinister.

On the agreed date I donned my good suit and travelled to the pub. I was met by a couple of chaps who were casually dressed and I was made welcome with a drink and a ham roll. It wasn't exactly how I expected any job interview to start. Anyway, they described their set-up and advised me of my job description.

I learned that they were Directors of an in-house company that managed an estate on the banks of the Thames. Their jurisdiction comprised an estate of detached houses, several blocks of up market self-contained two and three bed apartments, a club house and a marina. About six hundred properties, all freehold.

The whole development had once been a railway goods yard linking the Thames to the Grand Union Canal, but this was closed as a shipping terminal in 1964 and the housing estate was built on the resultant brown site between 1972 and 1978.

It transpires that the existing boss of the management company had resigned, leaving his position vacant. I was to be the Estate Manager for a probationary period of six months, with an option to become the full-time manager at the end of my probationary period. I jumped at the opportunity and, to show my appreciation, I bought another round of drinks and ham rolls.

I had forgotten that my grown-up rogue gene had been listening.

On the 17 August 1998, I travelled to work. Deliberately arriving about one hour early I took a leisurely stroll around the estate to familiarise myself with its layout. I realised that this was going to be a challenging job, but a job, nonetheless, that I considered I could cope with.

I then went to the management office to be welcomed by all the company Directors.

After a brief introduction I was taken to the staff room to be introduced to my workforce. I gave a brief speech about how I looked forward to working with them all, etc., etc., and then returned to sort out my office.

The next couple of months turned out to be turbulent, to say the least.

I found that the estate was beset with problems. Infrastructure problems, parking problems, inadequate staffing problems, staff attitude problems, health & safety problems, noise problems and vandalism and graffiti problems. The complaints were relentless and I found myself spending more time fire-fighting these than anything else.

I spoke to a Director about this and was uncomfortably edified by his comments. Not dissimilar to the Houses of Parliament, the residents were split into two warring factions; the pro ex-manager camp and the anti-ex-manager camp. The complaints, I learned, had almost tripled since the ex-manager had resigned and most of these complaints emanated from his camp.

There was to be an estate election in a few weeks' time. This election had been called by the residents to determine which Directors should be voted in to run the company. The Director I was speaking with admitted that his fellow Directors wanted a temporary manager to fend off the complaints until after the election. I was troubled by the fact that I had not been told about the election during my interview.

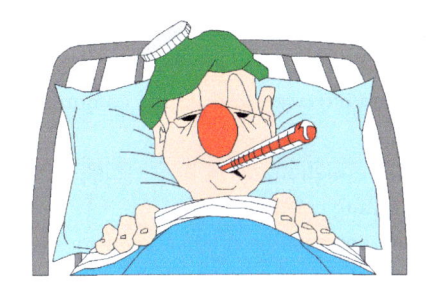

To make life even more complicated, I developed a severe elbow bursitis (Olecranon Bursitis) and had to be hospitalised with a life threatening infection caused by an insect bite.

My lower right arm swelled so much the fingers of my hand literally disappeared, melded together by my swollen dermis. My arm and hand looked like a huge sausage protruding from my elbow and the infection attacked almost every one of my internal organs... I really was in a bad way for a while!

After almost two weeks, gallons of intravenous anti-biotics and not much food, I was released back into the populace. My arm had deflated to its normal size and my fingers re-appeared, all present and correct.

Returning to work I had to organise the estate's voting procedures and polling station.

The election was held.

Spoiler alert! My grown-up rogue gene had recovered from his respite hospital care and was invigorated with new life... And a desire to punish me for making him ill.

The Directors of the existing management company were outnumbered by the pro ex-manager's camp and many were voted out of office, replaced with a selection of chums from the ex-manager's elite.

The ex-manager was immediately reinstated and he turfed me out of "his" office and wanted me demoted. I wasn't demoted, in fact, because I resigned before I suffered the ignominy of being demoted.

Much to grown-up rogue gene's pleasure I was, once more, unemployed.

I had "enjoyed" a mere three months in that job.

**

January 1999

I had just spent a couple of months visiting a myriad of employment agencies and I got a call from one that I'd visited in central London.

A firm of international human resource consultants needed an Office Manager to stand in for a chap who had had to take some sick time off work. With nothing to lose I went for an interview and started commuting to Chelsea.

This job turned out to be a positive nightmare! A bigger nightmare, even, than my last job managing a housing estate.

Shortly after starting my temporary contract the original manager died and I was offered a permanent position. Like an idiot I took the job.

With a degree in Facilities Management, membership of the Chartered Institute of Arbitrators, a wide-ranging knowledge of building construction and defects, and extensive experience in insurance claims management you would think that some respect would be bestowed upon me. Not so.

Okay, I know that you have to earn respect, but from the time I started as the full time manager I was perpetually walking around on the bottom of someone else's shoe. Let's just take a brief look at what I was up against...

The Finance Director, my immediate boss, had few interpersonal skills (in my opinion). He was a bully and constantly found fault in his staff's work, sending them away to "Do it again!" He frequently reduced one of his staff to tears. He almost reduced me to tears! He seemed to have an attitude of "I'm the only one that can do this job" but I've come across this type of boss in the army so I could handle the guy's criticisms.

The art was to keep going away to "Do it again", and after about three or four failures, he would do the job himself. I passed this gem of an idea on to a couple of the other members of his staff, who promptly adopted the plan. The guy finished up doing almost everything himself but at least he was happy with the end product. One could ask who was managing who?

Next, the Department Managers.

Now, we all had our budget to stick to. This wasn't new in the annals of worldwide department management but what was frustratingly annoying was the fact that that the other department managers seemed to regard my department budget as an extension of their own.

Because they wanted to show savings on their own budget they included stuff as a deduction for my budget that was nothing to do with me. No wonder they always showed a profit... On paper anyway! I had an annual battle isolating the stuff that they had heaped onto my budget, reversing this back to theirs just for me to break even. What an exasperating game this was! The Finance Director always asked why I had not made any savings.

What about the remainder of the staff? The Oiks. Those who had no promotional prospects but worked like dogs just to be able to afford their annual rail ticket home.

They had absolutely no concept of economical purchasing. They had to have the best of everything. The best quality paper for their paper aeroplanes, the best quality notebooks with lined pages to doodle in during the department managers' meetings, the best up-market chair with a head rest for their lunch time power nap, the most expensive kettle to boil their water for their pot noodles and not just any pencil... The pencils had to be the best retractable lead pencils that money could buy. Any suggestion of a normal HB pencil would harvest gasps of horror and invoke a meeting with the Managing Director to complain about their working conditions. Inevitably, I was instructed to give them what they wanted. So again, I ask who was managing who?

After three years, four months, three weeks, three days, four hours and thirty-five minutes I'd had enough. I resigned.

CHAPTER TWENTY

Bill's Farewell to the Treadmill

It is now May 2002.

I'm fifty two years old and I've never really settled down to being an employee in civvy street. Too many rules, too much commuting, too political and too much back-stabbing. Just like being in the army, eh? I didn't miss the army, but I did miss the banter of the blokes in it.

Being an employee reminded me of a quotation that I'd heard somewhere; 'The more people I meet, the more I like my dog.'

I was not going to re-visit the soap dispenser with tickets hanging from its arse again. I'd made my mind up about that.

After deliberating about my future I again reached the conclusion that self-employment was still the best way forward. But what could I do to generate a decent income? Fortunately, my wife was still bringing in the bread so we had no immediate urgency in finding a second wage. But my pride, again, wouldn't let me be a "kept man".

Having discussed the situation with my wife we came to the conclusion that if I was to go self-employed I would need re-educating to bring me up-to-scratch with legislation. So back to school I went.

I invested in several individual courses at RoSPA's head office in Birmingham, each about one week in duration with examinations at the end:

- DSE (Display Screen Equipment) inspection and user training.
- Employee Manual Handling training.
- Food Hygiene.
- Fire Risk Assessment and Prevention.

To enhance these courses I then invested yet more of our savings in a NEBOSH Certificate course (The National Examination Board in Occupational Safety and Health), again via RoSPA's head office. This one lasted for about three weeks, and again with a mega-exam at the end of it.

Once more I was the oldest student on every one of these courses but I didn't mind being mothered by the young ladies who insisted on paying for my lunchtime coffee. Having become an educated idiot in several disciplines I now felt that I could confidently re-join society as a Health and Safety (H&S) Consultant, training company employees in the art of Occupational Health and Safety.

My grown-up rogue gene hadn't interfered too much with my re-education. I say "too much" because there was an incident during my Manual Handling training that created a huge laugh for my class mates.

At the end of this course there were both written and practical exams. The practical test was the time when each student demonstrated his/her teaching technique to the course instructor.

Now, the art of lifting something off the floor without straining your back is to bend your knees and squat down without bending your back. This is analogous to a toddler squatting down to pick up a toy. Picture it. If you've got kids you'll know what I mean. If you haven't got any kids, get some. They're lovely... Until they become teenagers! That period in one's life deserves a whole library of books to explain the mindset of a teenager!

Anyway, my Manual Handling practical test was moving along smoothly and I could see that I was impressing everyone with my new-found knowledge of the subject. I squatted down to lift a cardboard box with bricks in it and it was at this point that my grown-up rogue gene decided to entertain the class.

Rrrrrrrip! My trousers split. Not just a little rip but a massive one. A catastrophic one.

The seam split from my zip all the way round to my belt. I stood up and looked sheepishly at the instructor who stared back as if to say, "What was that?"

With my back to the class somebody behind me said, "Sounded like he's just farted," raising titters from the class.

"No," I replied, "My trousers have just split," at the same time bending down to expose my underpants in all their glory.

The class and, may I add, the instructor all burst into fits of belly laughs as I stood there with a resigned smile on my face. One of the women commented "Red for Danger!" referring to the colour of my pants and raising more uncontrollable fits of laughter.

The instructor allowed me to go get changed into my tracksuit bottoms and I thanked my lucky stars that my grown-up rogue gene had not manufactured a more embarrassing scenario. I did, however, pass that exam with honours.

On return from my schooling I immediately set about forming my own company.

I designed and posted my web site for all to admire and I peddled my wares around various organisations. The response was good and I donned my suit, packed my briefcase with lined pads, pens and equipment, purchased film for my camera and filled the car with petrol. I was, once more, on the road travelling around the country inspecting offices and training staff.

I enjoyed every minute. I felt that teaching was my forte in life and this job brought back fond memories of the time I was an instructor in the army. I had some important clients; British Gas, Capita and Heart Radio to name a few.

Another quotation comes to mind here; "Those that can, do. Those that can't, teach."

Looking back on my whole life to this point, I think that by now I've shown that not only can I 'do', I can also teach!

***

If I've learned one thing during my civvy life, it is this... You cannot trust anybody. It's true. This mantra was reinforced during one of my fire risk assessments at an office somewhere in London.

One of the firms on my list of potential clients was a company that installed and serviced fire extinguishers. Let's call them 'Z'.

They didn't have anyone qualified to provide training or risk assessments in any way.

Having given my sales patter to Z's MD I left his office in the high hopes that he would appoint me to provide his company's H&S training. A couple of weeks later he called me back to his office with a proposal that he said would interest me.

The proposal was attractive; whenever Z's company attended one of their clients' offices to service the fire extinguishers the client would be encouraged to have a fire risk assessment carried out, with me as the risk assessor.

Back then it was a legal requirement for companies to have a fire risk assessment (I think it still is) and if they agreed to have one, I would be provided with the client's contact details to make an appropriate appointment. So, I would turn up in my own name and in my own company's capacity.

The risk assessment having been completed I would send my invoice to Z for payment.

I travelled up and down the UK carrying out the risk assessments, sometimes spending as much as a week away from home travelling from one client to the next. What I didn't know at the time was that Z's MD was charging the client twice, sometimes three times the amount I was invoicing him. I found this out when one of the clients mentioned that my fee for this work was very high.

Puzzled, I replied, "Oh? I didn't think that three hundred pounds was all that high. It's a reasonable sum."

"I agree, but you are charging nine hundred pounds."

"No, I invoice Z three hundred pounds for every one of my inspections."

"Well that's not what Z is charging us. Are you saying that if we appoint you direct you would charge three hundred pounds only?"

"Yes. That's correct."

"Okay, next year we will contact you direct."

I thanked him and with that we parted company and I made a note on my file to contact the client at the appropriate time to remind him it was time for his annual fire risk assessment.

Grown-up rogue gene saw this as an opportunity to drop me in it, big time.

Over the following year I must have done over two hundred risk assessments, some for myself, some for Z. I always diarised the date when a follow-up risk assessment was due and at the appropriate time I sent out my reminder letter to the clients. Some responded immediately to make an appointment with me.

Z's MD had also diarised some of the same clients to remind them that an inspection of their fire extinguishers was due and whilst on site, refurbishing fire extinguishers, Z mentioned the client's annual fire risk assessment. Inevitably, the client informed Z that they had already made an appointment with me to have one carried out.

On hearing this Z's MD got annoyed. Really annoyed! The boss called me to his office to shout and rant and rave at me that I was poaching his clients. Now, there are a few points here that Z's boss chose to ignore...

1. I wasn't poaching clients, they were still Z's clients in respect of maintaining the fire extinguishers.
2. Z did not own the client. It was the client's prerogative to appoint whoever they liked to carry out a fire inspection and Z had no say in the matter.
3. Z was, in any event, greedily overcharging the client for work that they didn't do. They were riding on my back and they were making a huge profit at my expense.

All 'Z's' boss had to say to this was, "Well, they're willing to pay."

I put it to him that, "If that's the case I'll increase my charge to you to six hundred pounds per inspection."

This clearly wasn't acceptable to him and he threatened to take out an injunction to prevent me from approaching his clients.

My response to this threat was a nonchalant, "See you in court, then."

I never received any more appointments from Z and I never heard from Z's boss again.

However, the appointments I had made with all Z's clients were suddenly cancelled. I had absolutely nothing to hang my hat on, but I was pretty sure that I had been bad-mouthed and that 'someone' had persuaded the clients to go elsewhere. Why else would a whole load of clients cancel their appointments...? All in the space of a couple of days? It just doesn't work that way, does it?

I reckon that my grown-up rogue gene had a hefty input to that skirmish but I just had to sit back, take another bashing and get on with life.

Anyway, in 2004 I moved my family to Leighton Buzzard and that's where I've settled.

In 2006 I sat down with my wife and told her that I had had enough of the trials and tribulations of working life and that I wanted to retire.

Although I still had a further nine years before my official retirement age we both agreed it was okay. My wife continued to commute to her job in London for three days each week and I wrapped up my business and settled down to doing the weekly shopping.

I have frequently reflected on my employment years since retiring and right now, 2022, I keep asking myself "Where the hell has all the time gone?"

BOOK 3

HOLIDAYS

CHAPTER TWENTY ONE

Bill under Canvas

I love camping. Unfortunately, I can't do camping any more, for several reasons.

I don't have a tent for a start, but even if I did my age prevents me from sleeping under the stars. I've grown too accustomed to the simple pleasures in life like a soft mattress and clean sheets and a proper roof over my head and anyway, my wife went off the camping idea during our cruise down the Colorado River... More on this cruise later.

I digress.

My brothers and I frequently went camping in our two-man bivvy. In fact, on hot summer nights we four brothers took the tent out to the fields, flipped a coin for the canvas roof and two of us slept outside under the stars. One of our favourite camping spot was at a place called Ford. As its name suggests, Ford was at the bottom of a valley close to Eckington. It was an ancient crossing point for horse and carts because the river was at its shallowest at that location. We caught many tasty trout dinners from the river and spent the evenings lazily talking away the hours.

Another favourite place of ours was the Hope Valley, in Derbyshire. During the summer holidays we took the bus from Sheffield bus station, always on the front seats of the top deck so that we could marvel at the view as the bus chugged over 'The Surprise'. Called Surprise View, it is situated on the A6187, a twenty minute bus ride from Sheffield and it overlooks the whole valley where Hathersage is situated. A stunning view. You should visit it sometime... You won't be disappointed.

Anyway, we got off the bus in the centre of Hope, a beautiful name for a beautiful village.

Back in the day Hope village was just a single street with quaint shops, surrounded by farm land. A really charming village. My dad knew the owner of Lose Hill Farm. The guy was an old army pal of dad's and he always welcomed us kids with bread and cake, cooked by his wife, and fresh milk straight from one of his cows. We pitched our tent behind the farmhouse and the guy always paid us a visit while we slept to make sure we were okay.

The farmer put us to work with him. We could be helping him shear sheep, or milking cows, or bailing hay, or plucking chickens. If more than two of us visited him those unable to sleep in the tent slept in the hay barn. Really cosy.

The farm was situated on the hillside above Hope, the fields surrounding the farm and between the farm and the town being owned by dad's pal. Many acres of grassland where the farmer's livestock grazed, each field separated by drystone walls built over centuries of farm ownership. My eldest brother and I were often given the task of rebuilding a section of these walls knocked over by an amorous bull trying to get to a suitable mate, or a section that had collapsed when a sheep used it as a scratching post. There is an art to rebuilding drystone walls, an art which I picked up while helping eldest brother.

I recollect going to the market in Castleton with the farmer, one sunny day, to auction some of his stock. A great day with lots of ice cream and chocolate given to me by the farmers at the market.

Now, we've all read or heard about kids going scrumping apples, haven't we? Well, my younger brother and I decided to go scrumping one evening, while camping at Lose Hill Farm.

To reach the farm we had to walk from the town along a narrow access road to a footpath that meandered it's way up to the farm. The access road was bordered by pretty cottages, all with half a dozen apple or pear trees in their front gardens. Actually the cottages' front gardens were, in fact, their rear gardens because the cottages had been built facing away from the road for privacy, a feature that we scrumpers found to be advantageous.

Each mini-orchard had its own drystone wall to separate it from the road.

Younger brother and I cased each one of the orchards every time we passed by on our way up the hill to our tent. We chose two likely looking orchards, one with apples and the other with pears.

Waiting until darkness descended on the valley we made our way down the hill to the orchards we chose to raid. They were, conveniently, next door to each other. You'll never believe this, but our rogue genes had decided to make our scrumping tour difficult.

During our 'casing' assignment we could see the orchard trees heavy with drooping branches full of ripe fruit, just daring us to go pick a few apples or pears from their branches. That's why we chose them.

Unfortunately, the trees looked a lot different at night time. From the same vantage point on the road we couldn't see one apple or one pear beckoning us. Nothing for it, we had to climb over the drystone wall and gingerly approach the trees. On reaching each tree we still couldn't see any fruit hanging down. Nothing for it, younger brother just had to scale the tree to get closer to the fruit, but having been given a leg up by me he still couldn't see any fruit.

So, here's what we did...

Younger brother gingerly made his way to the end of the branch he was standing on and gently bounced up-and-down on this. Standing underneath I was suddenly bombarded by multitudes of apples that dropped from the undulating branch and landed on the ground with a chorus of thuds. A brilliant idea!

Younger brother carefully slid down the tree trunk and we filled our pockets with apples.

On to the pear tree.

Again I gave him a leg up so that he could reach the branches, and he tentatively made his way along a bendy branch. Nothing happened when he first bounced this branch up-and-down.

"Try it a bit harder," I whispered.

Younger brother bounced a little harder. Still no falling pears.

"A bit harder," I hissed, at which point he decided not just to bounce on the branch but to give it a hefty stamp-on. Holding a branch above his head he lifted his feet up and with an angry two-footed kick clobbered the lower branch... Which snapped from the abuse it was receiving!

The branch, followed by younger brother, landed on top of me and bounced off my shoulder onto the ground with a loud thump. In the chaos we heard a large dog barking madly from within the house. At least it sounded like a large dog, but we didn't hang around to find out. We both ran for the drystone wall but in the darkness we never saw it approach. With a wallop we both hit it head-on... and a section of the wall fell onto the path.

Scrambling over the debris we both ran up the hill as fast as we could leg it, and just before we turned off the path to our tent we dived behind a mound of earth to wait for anyone chasing us. Sat behind the mound we took stock of our scrumping and found that most of the apples weighing our pockets down at the apple tree had fallen out during our dash up the hill. All we had left were just two apples each from a couple of dozen...

We sat there, in silence, for about half-an-hour munching our two apples just in case we had been pursued, but no-one came after us.

After breakfast we went back down the hill to inspect the damage we had caused. To our surprise and horror we found that a length of about ten yards of drystone walling had tipped over onto the path! Feeling guilty, my younger brother and I went and knocked on the cottage door.

"Missus, do you know that your wall has collapsed?"

"Yes," the woman smiled, "it must have fallen over last night. Do you two boys want a bag of apples to take home...?"

I think those days were some of the best days of my life. Camping out with my brothers, working on Lose Hill Farm, exploring in and around Hope valley, climbing to the top of Mam Tor and visiting the Blue John and Peak Caverns.

At that time there was always lots to see and lots to do, but not very much scope for any nonsense from my younger rogue gene.

***

During my army days I lived in a tent on several occasions.

I enjoyed our Kenyan camping trip at Nanyuki, on the Equator, the most. Lots of lovely grub from a bubbling cauldron and the nights were pleasantly warm.

A few of my mates and I even had the opportunity to stay in a place called Treetops.

All you children out there may not know about Treetops, in Kenya. It is Kenya's oldest safari lodge and it is the place where Princess Elizabeth was staying with Prince Philip, Duke of Edinburgh, when she was told her father, George VI, had died. She effectively became Elizabeth II, Queen of England and of all of the Commonwealth, there and then.

The army band I was in played a gig for some Kenyan government dignitary and instead of paying us he organised a few nights stay in Treetops for several of the band members. I and some of my mates were the privileged few to be chosen to stay at this place. We got picked up and taken there in a tour bus, all part of the deal. Those that didn't get the opportunity to stay at Treetops were given a mini safari out in the bush.

Now, Treetops was, at the time, exactly as its name describes. It was a hotel built into the tree tops adjacent to a small lake. At that time there were just six rooms but it's probably been extended since then. One could sit out on the balcony sipping booze and slowly getting inebriated while watching elephants and monkeys and antelopes and other jungle animals visit the watering hole to drink.

A huge change from our nights under canvas back at Nanyuki, the best elements of this trip were the hot showers, together with the soft mattress and the delicious food prepared by a Michelin-starred chef... Not the curry and chips unceremoniously chucked onto our plates by the Battalion's non Michelin-starred Army Catering Corp cook.

The one thing we 'guests' really enjoyed, however, was sleep. We had all seen pictures of elephants and monkeys and antelopes and other jungle animals on the television, but in the hotel we could sleep to our hearts content, rising from our slumbers at mealtimes after an alarm call provided by the obliging hotel staff.

At two-thirty a.m. one morning we were all gently shaken awake by a member of the hotel staff whispering, "Leopard, Leopard." I got up, dressed and went outside to the viewing balcony.

I heard the poor guy getting tongue lashed by a few of the blokes who impolitely, in true army fashion, suggested that he should, "Go away...!"

I got a few blurry photographs of the Leopard perched in a tree about ten feet from the balcony, chewing away on a small antelope it had recently caught and dragged up the tree.

It gave the phrase 'road kill' a whole new meaning.

CHAPTER TWENTY TWO

Bill Messing About on the River

When the weather is fine you know it's the time
For messin' about on the river.
If you take my advice there's nothing so nice
As messin' about on the river.
There's big boats and wee boats and all kinds of craft
Puffers and keel boats and some with no raft.
With the wind in your face there's no finer place
Than messin' about on the river.
Tony Hatch / Les Reed
1965 - Pye Golden Guinea GGL 0355 LP
1968 - Marble Arch MAL 825 LP MESSING ABOUT ON THE RIVER

Courtesy of Frank Suess

Does anybody out there remember that song? If you do you must be an old fart like me 'cos I remember singing this when it was first released in 1965. I thought it a good way of introducing my boating escapades.

In 1889 Jerome K. Jerome wrote a book titled 'Three Men in a Boat'. What started as a serious travel guide turned into a humorous two-week boating holiday on the Thames chronicling the adventures of three men and a dog rowing from Kingston-upon-Thames to Oxford and back. There have been several film, television and stage adaptations of this book although I can't honestly say that I've seen any of them.

However, in 1966, at the age of sixteen years, I and an army pal decided to do exactly that. Row up the Thames. Two men in a boat and no dog.

I firstly went home to Yorkshire to spend a few day with my parents and to pick up the tent, together with a primus stove, that I and my brothers used during our school holidays. I may have told you this on occasion, but I'll just remind you anyway; Yorkshire is the centre of the Universe.

There, I've said it and I don't care if you disagree with me.

Anyway, my mate and I (we'll call him P) got transported to Pangbourne by P's dad and we hired a rowing skiff for the vast sum of seven pounds for the week. It took us a while to negotiate down from one pound and fifty pence per day but the guy eventually caved in and showed us how to pack our belongings in the boat so as to keep it balanced.

We had quite a lot of gear; two rucksacks, signed out of the army stores, full of our clothing, the tent with the primus stove tied to the tent bag, several blankets and two pillows that P's mum had provided, several gallons of paraffin (fuel for the primus) and numerous shopping bags full of food.

We tentatively boarded the skiff and the guy bid us a safe journey. He must have thought we were mad. We were not mad, just young and carefree.

Off we went, taking it in turns to row upstream. The one steering could rest, sat at the rear of the skiff facing forward while the one rowing sat in the middle travelling backwards. Our gear was stowed at the front. The rower had to trust the steerer to point us in the right direction.

Now, steering the skiff was by pulling on one of two ropes attached to the rudder. You pull the left rope to turn left and the right rope to turn right. You would think this was an easy concept to grasp, but P just couldn't get it into his head. We spent an hour and a half zig-zagging across the river and we must have travelled many times the distance we would have travelled had we been steered in a straight line. After the first one and a half hours we could still see the boatyard from which we had departed, one hundred and fifty yards from our present position.

Swapping seats to take one's turn on the oars was a bit iffy, to say the least. You don't know how difficult it is to change seats on a skiff in mid stream. We both had to stand up together, meet halfway to our new destination, hug each other as we passed by and then occupy our new seat, at the same time keeping our balance. All without losing our gear or, indeed, our oars. The skiff by this time had drifted back downstream for about fifty yards and we could see that this trip would be hard work getting almost nowhere. But so what, we were having fun.

After several close calls when the boat dangerously rolled to one side and we almost lost our balance, and our gear, we eventually got the hang of swapping seats.

We settled down to a routine that we were comfortable with. Two hours on, two hours off.

***

Back in those days we could travel in our working clothes. Demins, boots, putties, KF shirt and beret, with a rucksack over our shoulder. As long as we were properly dressed at all times the army didn't have any problems with this.

I regularly hitch-hiked from Aldershot to Sheffield when I went on leave. It was easy to get a lift dressed as a soldier and it was cheaper than buying a rail ticket. You stuck your thumb out and almost immediately someone would stop to ask where you were going. It wasn't until the Northern Ireland troubles got kicked off in the late '60s that the army put a stop to all soldiers travelling in uniform.

So there we were, P and I, dressed as soldiers rowing upstream in a skiff that was heavily laden with our gear. We pulled in to cook some lunch and sat on the bankside, enjoying our freedom from taking orders and bulling (cleaning) our kit.

As we sat there a group of twelve young army cadets ran up to us, snapped to attention and gave P and I a smart salute. Quite why they saluted us is anybody's guess 'cos we had nothing on our uniforms to show we were officers. I suppose these schoolkids thought it was the proper thing to do, but P and I graciously acknowledged their salutes by giving one in return. Their faces beamed with pride.

The tallest chap, I guess the one in charge of this unit, asked if there was anything they could do to help us. They were, apparently, on some kind of orienteering exercise and they had seen us noshing our tins of soup by the water's edge. The cadets stood as straight and as stiff as lamp posts, awaiting their orders, while P and I thought of some task we could set these eager beavers to send them on their way.

Abingdon was about a mile and a half further upstream and P stroked his chin in thought.

"Okay, chaps. See that boat down there?" says P, pointing to our skiff, "Do you think you can get it to Abingdon without losing any of our gear?"

"Yes sir," the leader pipes up. "We'll get right on it."

The leader orders the cadets to fall out and they all trot down to the skiff.

Now, given this task what would you do to get the skiff to Abingdon? You would row it there, wouldn't you? Not this bunch. They hauled the skiff out of the water, divvied up its contents between six of them and the remaining six lifted the skiff onto their shoulders and proceeded to march up the towpath towards Abingdon, our gear following on behind.

P and I were amazed at the cadets approach to this task. I sometimes wonder if any had progressed to a position of power in the army, given the enthusiasm and precision exhibited by these future soldiers. I sincerely hope so...

The skiff and our gear arrived at Abingdon safely and was successfully re-packed and launched in true naval tradition with an escort of proud army cadets giving it a salute and a rousing cheer. Onlookers didn't have a clue as to what was happening, but it didn't stop them joining in the cheering and hat waving as the skiff regally slid down the bank and into the water. Passing holiday cruisers sounded their horns in true ship launching celebration.

Grown-up rogue gene even joined in by having a celebration of its own.

Nobody had bothered to hang on to the mooring rope and the rousing cheers tailed off to an embarrassing silence as we watched our possessions, taken by the river current back in the direction it had just been carried from. The cadets were mortified. Their jaws dropped. With eyes wide open in alarm their gaze shifted from each other to the skiff, now too far from the bank to rescue, but P and I just laughed as we chased along the towpath after it. A passing cruiser caught up with it, in mid-stream and travelling many knots faster than P and I could run, and the cruiser kindly towed the skiff back to the towpath for us.

After much apologising and more saluting the cadets marched off to their next assignment, whatever that was.

***

After securing the skiff we pitched our tent, got our primus stove up and running and cooked some spuds and carrots to accompany the sausages we had fried on top of an oven tray donated by P's mum.

It was now beginning to get dark so after cleaning our plates and utensils we bedded down for the night. After all, an early start the next morning would stand us in good stead for our forthcoming day of rowing. We left our primus stove outside to cool off and to make room for our sleeping bags.

Perhaps now is a good time to explain to all you couch potatoes how a primus stove works.

Nowadays, campers take all sorts of equipment with them in the boot of their cars when they go camping, gas stoves being a luxury that we never had back in the day. To fry eggs and boil sprouts and make tea you had to have a primus stove and an empty biscuit tin. You turned the biscuit tin on its side, put in your steak & kidney pie, replace the lid on the tin and balance this on top of your primus stove. A great oven and yes, it did get hot. That's how an oven works isn't it? So one had to be extremely careful not to burn one's hands when lifting this off the primus. A towel is useful at this time.

So how exactly does the primus stove work?

Well, our primus used paraffin as a source of fuel, this being retained in the lower chamber. You fill the lower of the cups (the one about midway up the stem protruding from the paraffin chamber) with methylated spirit which you ignite. The idea here is that the burning meths heats up the curved pipes just above the meths cup. Just before the meths in the cup runs out you slowly pump the plunger a few times to create a bit of pressure in the fuel chamber. This has the effect of pushing liquid paraffin up the stem to be vaporised in the heated curved pipes feeding the burners atop the primus stove, and the resultant vapour ignites from the flaming meths. Once the main burner is up and running you pump up the pressure in the chamber to strengthen and maintain the cooking flame. It's easy when you know how.

One thing that must be borne in mind at all costs is that these types of primus stove run solely on paraffin. Nothing else works, at least not in the way you want it to work.

Back to our camping adventure.

P and I stirred from our slumbers nice and early to the singing of the birds and the warmth of the early morning sun on our tent. After washing the sleep from our faces in the river we started to prepare our breakfast of fried eggs, sausages, fried bread and hot tea... Inside the tent. This was the usual location for our breakfast cooking because it was sheltered from the wind and it also acted as our central heating unit. First thing to do was to boil some water for the tea. Without tea I think the army throughout the ages would have collapsed.

What we didn't realise is that while we peacefully slept, some brain-dead idiot lout had crept up to our tent and substituted the paraffin in our primus with petrol! His (or her) rogue gene must have had a silent conversation with mine to play a dangerous trick on P and myself.

Everything was fine until I pumped some pressure into the fuel chamber. Neat petrol was forced into the vaporising tubes which, by all accounts, was hot enough to vaporise paraffin but not hot enough to vaporise petrol. The hot neat petrol shot out of the burner and was immediately ignited by the burning meths. P and I were trapped inside the tent as a fountain of flaming petrol cascaded in front of the entrance and started to spread across the ground.

We had to think quickly. Without speaking we both stood straight up in unison, pulling out the tent pegs and covering us in a ghostly tent shroud. We jumped backwards to prevent the tent from catching fire and hurriedly fought our way out of the shroud. P kicked the burning primus into the river shallows, dousing the flames amid a hissing of cooling metal and steam. That primus would need some attention when we could get round to retrieving it.

After stamping on the flames on the ground to extinguish them we inspected the tent and our blankets for damage. Fortunately, there was none. We both wished we could confront the lunatic that had almost killed us, but that would be unlikely, given that he/her/they would probably still be tucked up in their nice cosy and safe bed.

The primus required a lot of cleaning before we could use it again so we decided to have a couple of jam sandwiches and a swig of Tizer for breakfast. Packing up our camp we continued to row towards Oxford once more.

Our journey home from Oxford, to Pangbourne, took less time and was an easier row than our upstream trip because the river current pushed us along. On the way downstream we gave a lift to five girls who had shouted to us from the towpath. The skiff was now so heavily laden that water was almost to the top of the gunnels. But we had a few laughs and we both got lots of kisses and hugs from the girls when we eventually pulled in to allow them to disembark.

That holiday was one of the best I can remember having. Lots of laughs and lots of adventures with a friend that I'll always treasure.

It also gave me a taste of river life that spurred me on to more adventurous holidays afloat.

CHAPTER TWENTY THREE

Bill's Introduction to Motor Cruising

After my trip in a skiff, I got the boating bug.

The following year, 1967, P and I decided to move up a rung on the ladder of 'messin' about on the river' by hiring a motor cruiser. We hired one for our Easter break.

All we had to deliver to the boatyard were our clothes and food. No tent, no primus, no biscuit tin oven and no hard work rowing against the flow of the river. Having a motor was sheer luxury. This trip, however, was not without its hiccups.

On taking over the craft we were given a thorough lesson in boat management by the boatyard manager. What to clean, what to screw down, what to check, etc., that kind of thing.

Now one of the important daily tasks that the manager had stressed to us was that we must ensure that the prop shaft grease nipple screw must be given at least two turns prior to setting off.

Oh, you've never hired a motor cruiser so you don't know what the prop shaft grease nipple screw is. I'll try to explain.

On most cruisers the engine is inboard, i.e. the engine is inside the boat's hull. Some motor cruisers, by the way, have an outboard engine attached externally to the rear end of the boat, the stern. Not this boat. This boat's engine was inboard.

Now, to connect the inboard motor to the propellor, which is outboard, a propellor shaft has to protrude through the boat's hull. This tends to create a problem. How do you allow the propellor shaft to turn freely while protruding through the hull without letting water gush into the boat? At the time, this problem was overcome by installing a circular collar to support the prop shaft where it protrudes through the hull. The gap between this collar and the prop shaft was then packed with grease to prevent water flowing into the boat. The grease was packed into the collar via a grease nipple, this being fed by turning a screw on a cylindrical plunger attached to the hull and connected by a semi-flexible tube. The screw was the most important daily tasks to remember... Without the grease pack, water flowed into the boat's bilge past the prop shaft and slowly sank the boat.

Okay. I'm sorry if that bit bored you but I thought you should know how my rogue gene had decided to give our boots a wash, along with the boat's carpet and most of the cooking utensils in the floor standing cupboards.

A complete breakdown in communication took place between P and I.

Although we both attended the boatyard manager's lesson, and we both knew that it was important to give the grease nipple screw a couple of turns every day, we both thought that the other of us was doing this. It became apparent that the screw had not been screwed for several days. Our mistake was that we didn't have a plan! Not very military in its non-conception!

We woke up one morning, swung our legs out of our bunks and very quickly found that the floor was not just wet, it was almost knee deep in water. Our boots floated around the cabin as if they were enjoying an early morning swim and P and I immediately entered panic mode as we paddled around the cabin to retrieve our floating pants, denims and socks.

We quickly donned some dry clothes and went to investigate why the boat was sinking.

After lifting the engine hatch to find the engine three quarters submerged a process of elimination confirmed that neither of us had screwed the screw since we had departed from the boat yard, some three days earlier.

Screwing this down until I could feel a resistance of grease being forced into the collar I turned the engine on and we both waited for about an hour while the bilge pump expelled the water from the boat. Panic job over we set about cleaning up the inside of the boat, now a muddy brown colour a third of the way up the cupboard doors.

Thanks, grown-up rogue gene...!

***

After our trench foot incident P and I agreed a plan to ensure that the grease nipple screw was screwed down every day.

After a late breakfast we continued our cruise upstream. Oxford, next stop.

We moored up in a pleasant field just off Heyford Hill Lane, Oxford. A nice quiet place close to some shops. Our clothes had, by now, dried on the roof of the cruiser so we were able to change back into our army working gear of boots, putties, denims, KF shirts and berets. Our boots would take a little longer to completely dry out.

What we didn't know was that this particular quiet place was frequented by the local louts who came to swim in the Thames, make camp fires and do what teenagers did when grown-ups were not watching.

Returning to our cruiser from a shopping trip laden with shopping bags full of biscuits, cakes, ready meals, chocolates, crisps and other nutritious rations we saw, through the windows of the cabin, a youth going through our belongings. Another youth stood on the aft deck with his head poking into the cabin. The youths were being watched by several girls and two other yobs from the bankside.

We nonchalantly walked up to the girls with their backs to us and shouted "Oi!"

The startled girls turned and parted for us to walk between them up to the boat. Our shout encouraged the youth inside the boat to show himself.

"What are you two doing?" Questioned P, both of us barring the way off the boat.

"Nothing."

"So if you're doing nothing why have you got my pullover in your hand?" I asked.

"Oh, I found it on the floor and was going to put it on the bed for you."

First point... That's a lie 'cos my woolly pully was in a drawer.

Second point... It's not a bed it's a bunk, moron.

"What were you doing looking through the cupboards," to one guy, "and what are you doing standing on our boat?" to the other.

"Nothing"

"Liars, the pair of you."

"What did you just call us?"

"You heard, the first time. LIARS!"

I could see this conversation getting out of hand, but decided that P and I could damage two of the guys before the other two joined in. We walked a couple of paces backwards and allowed the two on the boat to jump to the bankside. They stood there, chests out, breathing heavily and gesticulating with their clenched fists, ready to repel anything P and I did. Before the intruders sprang into action one of the girls said "D {youth's name}, don't do it!"

"Why not?" replied D.

"My uncle's got a hat like that. I think he did things in the war. What regiment are you in?" she asked P.

"The Parachute Regiment."

"D, come away. These guys will kill you. You don't stand a chance."

One of the other guys piped up, "I've read about that lot. They don't mess about."

In a moment of pregnant pause the two invaders dropped their guard and looked at the group for some inspiration... Just the opportunity P and I wanted. In unison we both whacked the guys on their noses and watched as one rotated backwards into the river and the other collapsed in a heap onto the turf.

In an erudite way the girl said, "Told you... "

P and I turned to face the remainder of the group. "Next?" I invited.

One youth held his palms up in submission and went to help a wet and embarrassed adolescent back onto the bankside. The group all turned and walked a sheepish walk away from the boat.

P and I checked our belongings and opened a packet of biscuits for lunch.

A little while later two of the girls returned. When we had previously met the group of youths at our boat I had privately homed in on these two girls, thinking they were the best looking out of all the other girls in the bunch. P and I looked at each other in puzzlement, wondering what the girls were up to.

Absolutely nothing. They had returned to chat and to have some biscuits and to, "Get to know us" a bit better.

We sat on the grass drinking lemonade and talking about school and the army. When it started to get dark one thing led to another and P and one of the girls went into the boat, leaving me and the other girl "exploring" each other under the stars.

When the girls left to go home, P and I discussed the possibility of the youths returning with reinforcements to create some damage to either us or the boat or both. We decided to go on guard duty, three hours on three hours off, to watch for the returning gang. We loosened the mooring pin for a quick getaway.

As it turned out, nobody came back.

***

All too soon it was time to turn round and head for the boat's home base at Pangbourne.

On the way downstream we moored on Andersey Island, adjacent to Abingdon Bridge, to replenish our supply of chocolate and biscuits.

Grown-up rogue gene had not yet finished with us on this trip.

Returning to our boat from the shops, there it was... gone! We looked upstream, we looked downstream. No sight of it. P pulled on my shirt sleeve and pointed across the river.

On the other bank guess who we saw laughing and sticking two fingers up at us. Yep, you're right. The two youths whose noses we had recently flattened. The mooring pin was still hammered into the bankside so we guessed that the village idiots had untied the boat and then done a runner across the bridge.

We went to the local police station to report our loss, on the way discussing the prospects of finding the youths to make a better job of their noses.

Most places had police stations in those days, and they were all manned stations. You could go into one at any time of the day, or night, to report something bad and you could be sure that something will be done about what you had reported. Sadly, not so today.

After making our report to the desk sergeant we were instructed to go back to the bridge and wait. We sat on the bank absentmindedly digging a hole with our one remaining mooring pin and we heard, "Hiya!"

Looking over our shoulder we spotted the two girls we had been with a few nights earlier at Heyford Hill Lane approaching us. They sat down and asked where our boat was. We told them. With looks of annoyance the girls gave us the youths' names and addresses. P disappeared under Abingdon Bridge with his girl from our last liaison and I sat with mine, just chatting and 'exploring' some more.

After maybe half an hour my chat was interrupted by a policeman who told us that our boat had been prevented, by a pleasure craft, from crashing down a weir and that it was moored up next to a lock about a mile downstream. I thanked the policeman and gave him the names and addresses of the youths who had released our boat. I then prised P from his girl. We said our goodbyes to the girls and we set off along the tow path to find our boat.

P and I vowed not to leave the boat alone from that moment onwards.

I never heard if the police took any action against the youths.

***

Once more in charge of the boat we again made our way home.

It was a smooth journey. Except, that is, for an incident in which I rescued a tiny tot from drowning.

I was driving the boat and I had decided to put its engine into neutral to save fuel and allow the midstream flow to silently carry us downstream. P went down to the toilet to relieve himself of the gallons of Cola he had drunk. I enjoyed the sight and sounds of the balmy summer afternoon. The sun glistening off the water. The birds singing. The distant chime of a church clock. Ducks quacking a laugh at us as we passed by them. The hypnotic rippling of the river against the boat's bow... And a woman screaming for help!

What? The tranquillity of our trip downstream was interrupted by a woman screaming in anguish.

Looking down the side of the boat towards the rear of the one in front of us I saw a young boy bobbing up and down and frantically splashing to stay afloat. We were heading straight for him so I slammed the boat's engine into reverse, steered to one side and shouted to P to "Get out here!"

I dived into the river to swim towards the child who had no life jacket on and who was beginning to spend more time under the water than above it. His mum was, by now, frantically waving her arms and hysterically screaming for someone to help.

Now, bear in mind that I had never, ever, had any kind of instruction about how to save someone from drowning. All I had to go on was what I'd seen on TV... Not a lot of help in a situation like this.

My clothes and boots prevented me from power swimming to the boy and I cursed them for slowing me down. Suddenly the boy was there, right in front of me, and I galvanized my effort to reach him. He was still thrashing about in the water when I reached him. This probably stopped him from sinking and I grabbed the front of his pullover and pulled him to me.

A mistake!

I've since learned that you should always try to approach a drowning person from behind because the first thing they do is try to use you... Your head specifically, as a convenient float to save themselves from going under. All that happens is that they push you under then follow you in a panic. If you're not careful you both die.

Taking a deep breath I pushed the boy away from me then caught his arm to turn him round. Pure instinct. As he turned his back to me I grabbed him round his chest with one arm and started to swim with my other arm towards the boat with the screaming woman on board.

A bloke bent over the side and lifted the boy back into the boat... And just left me there while he took the boy into the cabin! Hanging onto the side of the boat I shouted "Oi!" to no-one in particular and the woman's arm appeared over the side. I took her hand and she helped me climb into the boat.

She was all over me like an octopus, showing her gratitude by hugging me and kissing every inch of my face. The boy's dad reappeared and I sarcastically said, "It's okay. I managed to climb on board." He looked a bit sheepish for not giving me a hand.

The boy's mum laughed that she was now "All wet" from thanking me for saving her offspring, and that she should go below to change into a dry blouse. I graciously declined her invitation to follow her to get out of my wet clothes. I'm sure it was an innocent suggestion but I didn't feel inclined to take her up on the offer because I wasn't quite sure where that was going and anyway, the boy's dad was bigger than me.

I did, however, get a good eyeful as I watched the woman change her blouse just inside the doorway to the cabin. Bra-less, she looked up at me and smiled a wink at me while she was changing!

P pulled up alongside us to enable me to climb from one boat to the other. The parents thanked us both profusely for what we had done and we continued our journeys to the next lock and downstream to the boatyard. I re-joined P at the helm he told what had happened after he heard me shout, "Get out here!"

I had caught him with his trousers down and he apparently thought I had called him to go look at something interesting. It was interesting all right. I had left the boat in reverse gear when I dived into the water. When he eventually emerged from the W.C. he saw that the steering wheel was unmanned. Looking round in disbelief he saw me frantically swimming downstream away from the boat, fully clothed, and he suddenly realised that the boat was driving itself into the bankside uncontrollably. He had to slam the boat's gear into forward thrust to avoid a nasty collision. He didn't even see me save the boy and he didn't see the octopus hanging round my neck. All he saw was me waving to him from the other boat to come over and pick me up.

The rest of our trip downstream was uneventful and we arrived back at the boatyard with the boat in one piece and lots of yarns to relate to P's mum and dad. P's dad was a bit taken aback when he arrived to collect us from the boatyard when he saw me standing there, soaked to the skin and dripping water onto the path.

He didn't ask how or why I was soaked and dripping, he just suggested that I change into some dry clothes before getting into his car.

CHAPTER TWENTY FOUR

Bill's Cruise on the Norfolk Broads

I had got the boating bug big time.

Apart from a big ship sea cruise when JPC band (The Junior Parachute Company) got invited to do a gig on a cruise ship full of young students (more on this later), it was a few years before I went river cruising. But I always longed to get back onto a cruiser and enjoy the peaceful meandering of a river. In fact, it wasn't until I had been married for a couple of years that I persuaded my wife to join me on a holiday afloat.

I'm confident that many of you will have had a week or two cruising on the Norfolk Broads. It's great fun, isn't it? Taking in the fresh air and scenery at three miles per hour, what else can you do but relax? Although it's not without its mishaps. Especially if your grown-up rogue gene accompanies you on the trip. Mine did on the occasion that I visited this peaceful place with my wife.

I hired a cruiser from a boatyard at Horning, on the river Bure. Our plan was to cruise down the Bure to Great Yarmouth, then on to the River Yare before turning round at Reedham and heading back home.

It is usually about four p.m. when most boatyards release their boats to tourists. This is because the boatyard likes to clean and refuel the boats before handing them over, and it sometimes takes the time from handing in at between nine and ten a.m. until four p.m. to complete this housekeeping, specially if there are several boats to prepare. So when you have signed your boat out there is, perhaps, a couple of hours cruising time before you have to moor up for the night. A lot depends on the time of the year. In the summer months you have a little more time to enjoy yourselves before woofing down your tea and bedding down.

We decided to turn into Wroxham Broad on the way down the Bure. Although this place was quite near the boatyard, an early stop-over would give me time to do a bit of fishing while my wife cooked the tea.

My wife gingerly made her way to the bow to be ready to lower the anchor into the water after I had brought the boat to a stop. For those of you who have never been anywhere near a boat and don't know your cleat from your cockpit the bow is the sharp end of the boat, the pointy bit at the front.

Finding a convenient location in the centre of this huge lake I signalled to my wife to drop anchor. I watched as the anchor was given a couple of swings to get it away from the boat and she let go. Splash! The anchor dived under the water's surface and we both watched, in disbelief, as the end of the anchor rope followed the anchor and disappeared into the murky depths. Nobody had checked that the anchor rope was attached to the boat!

Bloody grown-up rogue gene had struck again.

We decided the best thing to do, under such circumstances, was to a find a convenient tree close by tie up to.

***

After a peaceful night's sleep we set off once more in the direction of Great Yarmouth. This time without an anchor. We would need to find a suitable chandler to purchase a replacement before returning the boat.

Now what we didn't know was that the rivers Bure and Yare are both tidal rivers. There are two distinct places where these rivers flow into the North Sea. The Bure flows to Gorleston-on-Sea where it joins the North Sea and the Yare flows to Lowestoft and out to sea further down the Norfolk coast. These two rivers converge at Great Yarmouth adjacent to the A12 at the junction of Acle New Road and Hall Quay Road. Now, when the tide goes out along the Norfolk coast the junction of the Bure and the Yare becomes a bottleneck for the outgoing tidal waters. We didn't know this either.

The Bure, at this location, was about thirty five feet wide. With limited mooring at Yarmouth we were lucky enough to get a parking place a little way upstream of the bridge over the river at Acle Road. The tide was incoming. We must have arrived at this location perhaps three to four hours before the tide was due to turn. We didn't know this. Grown-up rogue gene gave me a clue that he was up to no good because we had to stand on the roof of the boat to reach the bank and tie up. The river was about eight feet from the top of the concrete quayside.

A bloke with an official looking hat came up to us as I was securing the boat ropes and asked if we would like our ropes checked throughout the night. It would cost us a fiver. After a bit of thought I informed the chap that I would look after the ropes myself.

"Okay," he says. "Your choice."

What did he mean by that? I thought it was a no-brainer. Providing I made sure that the ropes were nice and secure what else was there to do? What "Looking after" did our ropes require?

The guy did say that we would need more slack on the ropes to account "... for the flow of the river." So I released a few feet of rope in compliance of his suggestion. He didn't mention the tide. Ultimately, we would need a lot more than ten feet of slack rope, but we didn't know this.

Something else we didn't appreciate is that all tides flow in six hourly cycles. It takes about six hours for the tide to come in, then the tide turns and it takes about six hours for it to go back out. Looking at our map of the river we assumed that this location, far away from the coastline, would be unaffected by the tides. Wrong!

Okay, picture this. It is about six in the evening and high tide wasn't due until about nine p.m. So the tide was about half way to its highest point and the river at our spot was gently flowing upstream under the bridge, back towards Wroxham 'cos the tide was still coming in.

We didn't know this.

Having tied the boat to the quayside using the mooring rings embedded in the concrete paving we settled down to our tea, followed by a gentle walk around town and then to bed.

Something else we didn't know was that the tidal drop at this location, the distance from high tide to low tide, was a good fifteen to twenty feet!

The place where we moored up in Yarmouth, back then, has dramatically changed to what it is today. When we moored there the width of the river was, as I said earlier, about thirty five feet wide. At low tide the river Bure rushed under the bridge at a really fast rate of knots and it's almost impossible to motor against the flow at that location, so holiday cruisers just waited it out until the tide turned and water started to flow upstream once more.

The speed of the outgoing tide at the bridge was like pulling the plug on a dam across the width of the river. It was even too dangerous to cruise in the direction of the flow because the speed of the water interfered with steering and there was a great danger of colliding violently with moored craft.

At about midnight we were woken from our slumber by a commotion upstream. Lots of blokes shouting and women screaming and I went outside to see what all the noise was about.

The tide had turned at about nine thirty p.m. and our boat's roof was just below the level of the quayside path. In the distance I could see a pleasure craft charging, unimpeded, towards me. It spun uncontrollably as the fast river current carried it downstream with the outgoing tide.

On the quayside I noticed a bloke sprinting towards the bridge in an attempt to catch up with the unrestrained craft.

It was obvious that something, or someone, had released the craft from its mooring. At that time of the morning there could only be one of two reasons for this. Either someone had not tied the mooring ropes securely to its quayside mooring rings and the craft had slipped its mooring, or someone had untied the ropes and let the craft loose. I, personally, would bet on the latter.

Anyway, the running bloke suddenly changed his mind about reaching the bridge and turned towards the river. Dashing across the roof of my boat he made a flying leap towards the uncontrolled craft which was, by now, charging past mine after bouncing off several other crafts moored upstream. This turn in direction by the bloke was inspirational. If he had tried for the bridge he would have missed the speeding boat. On the other hand, if he had mistimed his leap he would have landed in the fast flowing river current and been carried downstream, with little chance of survival.

But he had timed his leap to perfection, colliding with the side of the spinning craft and clutching a grab rail on its roof. Climbing on board I saw him dash into the cabin and reappear with the craft's ignition key. As the craft disappeared under the bridge I heard its engine roar into life. I guess that the guy must have somehow gained control of the craft before it was taken out to sea with the tide.

That guy was an extremely brave person!

***

My wife and I returned to bed.

As soon as our heads hit the pillow once more we were gone... Dreamland, that peaceful nothingness of relaxing sleep. But grown-up rogue gene never sleeps, does it? It waited until we were somewhere on a distant planet and snoring, then devised a way to disturb us.

I woke at about one thirty a.m. Correct me if I'm wrong, but isn't the boat a bit lop sided? Nah, it's nothing. Go back to sleep.

At one forty-five a.m. I felt myself rolling towards the edge of the bed. That confirmed it. The boat was definitely on a slant.

I quickly pulled on my trousers and pushed on my shoes and went outside to investigate the reason for this unequal pitch. To my horror I found that the side of the boat had hooked onto the quayside. The ropes were preventing the boat from lowering with the outgoing tide and the water was quickly draining from under the keel as the tide receded. I had to somehow get the boat unhooked from the quayside and release more rope to allow the boat to lower with the tide. That's what the guy with the hat was on about!

Pulling on the rope did no good. It was now taking the full weight of the one ton boat and I was concerned that the rope cleats would get pulled from the boat hull. I couldn't reach the top of the quayside so I was effectively marooned on the boat, now beginning to creak under the strain of hanging by its ropes and listing heavily to one side. I heard some of the crockery tip out of the cupboards and I started to get really concerned about the situation.

I tried prising the boat off its hook with the barge pole. No joy. Although this pole was about two inches thick it bent as much as I dared to bend it without it snapping.

Placing one foot against the quayside and standing on the deck I took a deep breath, pushed with my bankside foot and heaved with my hands wrapped around the gunwales. This was an extremely dangerous manoeuvre. I knew that there was a possibility that my fingers could be trapped between the boat and bankside, and probably sliced off if the boat lurched from its hooked up position. But this, I felt, was a risk worth taking to protect the boat and, indeed, my wife who had not yet rolled out of bed and continued to snore in innocent oblivion to what was happening. I didn't want one of the cleats collapsing and upending the boat on the other rope.

I would just have to get my hands out of the way in time.

The first heave didn't budge the boat and I was beginning to get seriously worried. 'Try and try again' has always been my boosting mantra whenever rogue gene has brought life to a standstill. This mantra had now become a battle of wills between grown-up rogue gene and myself in the fight to release the boat.

The tide was still receding.

My wife appeared in the cabin doorway to tell me that the boat was on a slant...

After several attempts to free the boat, grown-up rogue gene gave up the fight, and with a mighty heave by me the boat suddenly unhooked from the quayside and dropped into the water with a mighty splash. Instinct had made me let go of the gunwales at exactly the same time as the boat released from its hook and I fell backwards and lay on the deck, having banged my head against the opposite side of the boat.

However, I could not yet rest on my laurels. Looking at my watch it was about two-fifteen a.m. The boat was now too far down in the water to reach the top of the quayside but I knew that I should stay awake anyway, paying out the mooring ropes as the tide receded.

I sat there, exhausted, with blistered hands and a bump the size of an egg on my head, but at least I had won one hell of a battle with my grown-up rogue gene.

***

Excitement over for the night, I continued to pay out my mooring ropes as necessary until the tide turned at about three-thirty a.m. I sat there, dozing, as the incoming tide gently raised the boat to a level that would enable me to jump onto the quayside.

After a modest breakfast of scrambled eggs, bacon, sausages, fried bread, mushrooms, baked beans and gallons of tea we made our way downstream once more.

I hadn't forgotten about our missing anchor. At the first opportunity I decided to moor up to a landing stage adjacent to a chandler's shop on the river Yare. As I approached this I misjudged the speed that the boat was travelling and its bow dived under the landing stage.

The boat came with a small triangular flag fashioned in the pattern of the owner's brand. It was attached to a flagpole sticking out of a receptacle at the front of the bow.

The flagpole was about as thick as a broom handle. It stood absolutely no chance of bringing the boat to a halt as the bow dived under the landing stage, and the pole snapped. The bit with the flag still attached fortunately dropped onto the bow deck.

The flagpole was now considerably shorter than when we first set out but I poked the stump back into the receptacle having firstly ejected the lower length of broken flagpole. It looked a bit stupid with the flag now flapping on a pole about two inches in height above the bow, but we hoped that nobody would notice.

As it happens, the chandler's shop didn't have an anchor of the same type as the one that we had thrown away so we decided to keep quiet about it when we handed the boat in. If anybody noticed it was missing we would just have to lose our deposit, but in the event nobody said a word.

Our adventures on the Broads didn't put us off boating and my wife and I continued to hire river cruisers for several years.

CHAPTER TWENTY FIVE

Bill's Family Cruise on the Thames

If I've learned one thing during my passage through life's rich patterns of ups and downs it is this; NEVER take your relatives on holiday with you. Don't!

At least, not until you've reserved a bed in the nearest state mental institute. It's not worth the damage to your nervous system or the probability of becoming addicted to nail biting. Don't do it! I took my parents on a cruising holiday on the Thames once. This trip turned out to be a laugh a minute... For my grown-up rogue gene, anyway.

From the moment I signed for the boat at Hampton my dad took over the helm and flatly refused to hand it over. Like a guardsman on sentry duty he took up position in front of the helm even as the boat owner was running through all the boat instructions with me. I had to unload the car and hump all the suitcases and bags of supplies from the car park on my own 'cos he insisted on guarding the helm to prevent anybody from muscling in on it. The message was clear. He was going to steer the boat for the whole of this trip. I couldn't even beat him to it first thing in the morning. Whatever time I decided to get out of bed he was there before me. It was as if the alarm clock in his head woke him a good ten minutes before mine. He even ate his breakfast stood up in front of the steering wheel!

Dad in the Royal Horse Artillery (1944)

And what about Mum? Well, she loved cooking, and in any other circumstance she was a fantastic cook. Her pièce de résistance was her meat and potato pie. The trouble was that she couldn't get used to the calor gas oven. These types of ovens are prevalent in the leisure cruising industry but they are not as efficient as the natural gas ovens we have in our homes. Consequently, chefs have to allow more time to cook food, or pastry turns out to be a soft mush on the inside with a slightly crusted skin on the outside, and all meat had to be returned to the oven for another hour because it came out really bloody and full of growing bacteria. Appetizing, eh?

So, what can I tell you about this week of nerve clattering episodes that I've tried to forget? Let's start with dad's driving...One rule of the river is that you always pass an oncoming boat on the right hand side of the river. You can steer down the centre of a river if there is no-one approaching you from the direction you are travelling, but you never travel on the left. Stay on the right or in the middle. Another rule is that you stay away from anglers' fishing rods. Anglers get fed up with leisure boats continually passing their pegs because they disturb the fish and chase them away.

One problem here is that fishing poles can reach across to the opposite river bank, so it's always advisable to slow the boat and steer down the centre of the channel when passing men fishing from the bankside. That way everybody stays happy and the anglers with fishing poles raise their rods in a kind of salute as you pass underneath. If there is a row of several fisherman's poles it's like emerging from a church wedding with your comrades in arms providing the guard of honour. All the poles go up at once as you regally pass under them.

I fully briefed dad on these rules as we set off in the direction of Oxford.

One blissful morning the sun was shining from a cloudless sky and the air had a spring-like feel. A cooling breeze brushed our hair back and my mum and wife were comfortably ensconced on the seats of the bow deck gossiping about nothing in particular.

I had taken up my usual position next to dad to keep an eye on his driving. Either my grown-up rogue gene or dad's grown-up rogue gene must have got bored because I had to leave dad on his own while I went to visit the toilet inside the main cabin. A bad call...

As I stood in the toilet compartment relieving myself of the gallons of tea that I'd had at breakfast I heard a proper commotion though the toilet window. Things bounced off the window and there was the scrape of other things brushing against the hull.

I heard Mum shout, "Bill!" in urgent tones.

Now, all you blokes out there know that you just cannot disturb your flow in mid-stream without some penalty. Usually, the penalty of coming to an emergency stop is to drench your leg in unfinished wee-wee, and that's exactly what happened to me. Ignoring the damp patch on the left thigh of my trouser leg I pulled up my zip... Too fast, and caught my foreskin in the zip's teeth! All blokes have done this at some time or other and I can tell you it's bloody painful! But the commotion outside was now sounding a bit urgent. I decided to leave well enough alone as far as the zip was concerned and with my trouser fly half done up, my shirt tail hanging out to cover my crown jewels, I went out to see what on earth was going on.

I was met by a shower of maggots, sandwiches, sweetcorn bait, lumps of cheese, tomatoes, slices of bread and a barrage of verbal abuse interspersed with the foulest of language, all directed at us from the bankside on our starboard (right hand) side.

I turned to look forward and saw utter chaos as the boat ploughed through and demolished a row of about a thirty fishing rods and poles, carefully placed on rod holders by the anglers who had stood back to have a chat amongst themselves.

The speed we were travelling would have easily won us a cup and a bottle of champagne to squirt everywhere at Monaco Grand Prix! Behind us was a scene from a demolition derby, with rods and poles scattered and sinking into the muddy brown water, disturbed by the boat, and with several more being dragged along because their hooks had snagged somewhere on the boat's keel. The air was erupting with angry expletive bellows from the anglers with raised fists who continued to throw anything to hand at us.

I shoved dad to one side, throttled back from full revs and spun the helm anti-clockwise to steer us away from the bank, narrowly missing several more rods. The rods we had been dragging behind us disappeared into the murky depths as their lines snapped.

I didn't think an apology would suffice, so I motored on until I thought we were safe enough away from the carnage to stop and release my foreskin from its detention. That was bloody painful, as well!

I tackled dad about the massacre we had just left behind us.

"What were you thinking? Couldn't you have avoided them? Why were you travelling so fast?"

I suppose he had a point of sorts when the response he gave was,

"Well, they should have seen us coming. Anyway, you told me to drive on the right."

Although that was hardly an excuse for the bloodbath that we had just left in our wake, we all know that it is difficult for a Yorkshireman to accept any kind of responsibility for his actions...

We spent six days motoring upstream, some of the time with dad embarrassingly bellowing abuse at other boaters

"You're too close," or...

"You're too fast," or...

"You're too noisy," or...

"Move over."

Some pedestrians on the towpath enjoying a peaceful walk arm-in-arm and minding their own business also felt the sharp end of his tongue when he glared at them and menacingly growled, "What are you looking at?"

Whenever another boat approached ours or whenever we were close enough to the towpath to communicate with strangers, which was all too frequent for comfort, I ducked back into the cabin to hide my face and let dad rant, unaccompanied, at the poor unfortunates.

After almost a week I was glad to turn round and head back to the boatyard.

***

After a while I was sufficiently confident that dad could handle the steering on his own so I spent much of the time reading or socialising with Mum and my wife, all of us sat comfortably on the bow seats.

In dad's quiet moments the journey was peaceful. The birds sang, the weather was balmy and the gentle splash of the river against the bow helped us all to relax. What else could one do but relax when the maximum speed on the river was between three and five miles per hour. A gentle stroll, by all accounts.

Dad shouted, "Bill? Have you got a minute?" I went to see what he wanted.

I poked my head out of the cabin and asked, "Problem?"

"No, not really. I was just wondering why the bloody river has disappeared."

Okay, a brief pause here to explain why most rivers and canals throughout the world are essentially considered as 'controlled waterways'. The contours of land vary in height so to overcome the effects of the uneven drops in the flow of water, locks were invented to raise and lower boats, ships and other watercraft between stretches of water of different levels.

Now, most people think that locks were invented during the industrial revolution in the 1800s. Not so. They have been around for much longer. Locks were first used in China during the Song Dynasty (960 – 1279 AD), having been pioneered by the Song politician and naval engineer Qiao Weiyue in 984 AD.

The lock designer knew that stemming the flow of water at any given location would create a flood, so weirs were constructed adjacent to locks to allow the river to continue its passage unimpeded when the lock was in use. A weir, or low head dam, is a barrier that alters the flow of water and usually results in a change in the height of the river level, sometimes producing drops of many feet. There are many weir designs but, fundamentally, water flows freely over the top of the weir crest before cascading down to a lower level.

On the River Thames, generally, a junction in the river has been engineered to divert the water from the locks to the weirs to prevent flooding of the locks, so in many cases one makes the decision to take a left or right channel in the river to approach the lock. Appropriate directions are provided for boaters to make the correct decision.

Got it? If I've not been clear enough for you to get the picture, search the internet for 'waterway locks' for a better explanation and, indeed, some pictures for those of you who can't read.

Okay, back to my cruise with dad at the helm. Where was I?

Oh, yes, dad had just casually made a most profound statement; "... I was just wondering why the bloody river has disappeared."

This comment didn't sit right with me. Rivers just don't disappear when one is lazily cruising on them, do they?

Yes, they do if you are rapidly approaching a weir!

With a puzzled expression on my face I climbed the steps of the cabin to stand on the deck and look in the direction of travel. To my horror the boat was about fifty feet from the edge of a weir, with dad oblivious to the oncoming danger posed by the drop in water level.

With a panicked shout of "No!" I barged dad out of the way and slammed the engine into reverse to stop the boat's forward motion... Don't forget that boats do not have emergency brakes in the same connotation as driving a car! All I could do was to watch as the boat approached the weir's overflow.

As if it could hear me, I gave repeated instructions to the boat to "Slow down, slow down, slow down... "

I've made the following comment before, but 'damage me, damage my rogue gene.' So my grown-up rogue gene must have acquiesced to this refrain and it stopped the boat with about five feet to go to the edge of the weir. With a huge breath of relief I waited as the boat slowly began its trajectory in reverse.

After reversing the boat back to the main channel and pointing it in the direction of the oncoming lock I turned to ask dad what the hell he was thinking of.

With a look of puzzlement, and hands upturned, he just said, "What...?"

After just two weeks I vowed never to take my parents on another boat.

Like an idiot I ignored this vow in later years.

***

In fairness dad had many redeeming features. He was always at the front of the queue to help people and he always gave his best to everything he did.

He never gave up on anything. An example of this is the time we were cruising along one of the canals. After a stormy night we came across a tree that had been blown over and was laying prone across the canal, blocking the passage onwards. The tree was being inspected by boaters, walkers and a few locals from a nearby pub, all giving advice about what to do to get the canal unblocked. There was quite a queue of narrowboats waiting to continue with their journeys.

Someone produced a handsaw to remove the branches overhanging the towpath. Dad watched as several of the bystanders sawed and sweated and laboured at trimming the branches. Ultimately, the huge tree trunk with a diameter of about one metre still blocked the channel.

Having laboured so much, the men in the group stood back to wait for somebody to suggest what to do next. Having sawed through a few branches they considered that they had done their bit for the day.

Do we wait for British Waterways to come and remove the tree? No good. That would take about a week and hired boats had to be returned to their boatyards before then.

Dad stepped up.

He inspected the rusty saw with very few sharp teeth then got stuck into the tree trunk. A couple of hours later and the trunk was sawn in half! Dad didn't stop sawing. With tenacity he just put his back into it until the job was done.

The people waiting to cruise onwards pulled the two halves of the trunk to one side while dad went for a shower. He didn't get any thanks. He didn't ask for any.

He understood the job that needed to be done and he just got on with it.

CHAPTER TWENTY SIX

Bill's Big Boats

Big boats. Big cruise ships, some in excess of fourteen floors high. A small town floating in the ocean. Now we're talking holidays.

There isn't much that can go wrong on a cruise ship. Not for the passengers, anyway. I love 'em, the holiday cruise ships that is.

Every five years I book a cruise on a big ship for our holiday. I choose the five year mark because it takes me that amount of time to save up for this type of holiday. And when I'm on board I make every penny count. Free drinks – yea! Lots of sun – yea! Lots of rest and relaxation – yea! Lots of delicious meals – Mmmmm! I usually put on about five or six pounds in weight during my holidays on the big ships, and it usually takes me five or six years to lose all that extra baggage but I don't care.

Even my grown-up rogue gene takes a break... Most times.

You may recall that I made a very brief reference to big cruise ships in chapter twenty-four. Well, my first ever big ship cruise took place the same year that I joined the army in 1962.

The band that I was in got a gig on a cruise ship full of final year, sixteen year old students on a ten day 'broaden your mind' trip to Vigo, Lisbon and Tangier, then back home. There were also several grown-ups on the ship, all teachers, supposedly looking after the students and making sure that the virgins remained virgins. They didn't do a very good job! The teachers had their minds on other 'broaden your mind' type activities as the boundaries between the teachers from different schools became somewhat blurred!

The ship docked in each port for a couple of days to enable the teachers and students to explore the surrounding towns and absorb some culture. The band played the ship out of the ports and performed concerts on deck while we steamed from one port to the next. I was in charge of the band's instrument stores so I had a key to this private place with a bunk and no windows.

The band had the pick of the girls on the cruise, constantly lining up to date them. Naturally, being the most handsome out of all the blokes in the band, I could show several of the girls how difficult a job it was to look after the instruments store with a bunk and no windows.

I think that this cruise was the one that permeated the boating bug in my veins and gave me a love of river and ocean cruising.

Cruise ships have absolutely everything one requires for a week or so of rest. What else is there to do but rest on these ships? You can't go anywhere until the ship docks in some foreign port, so you might as well relax and enjoy the cruise.

Most ships have several restaurants, a theatre, a cinema, a swimming pool, a gymnasium, a massage parlour, a doctor's surgery, shops, lots of shops, a casino, someone to make your bed and do your laundry and bring your drinks to you... Sheer decadence.

All this, however, comes at a price – usually several thousand dollars per person plus gratuities. It's worth it, nevertheless, just to lie back and be treated like royalty. Cruise ship companies really know how to treat people, and they make sure that the customer is always right.

So I don't really have any humorous anecdotes about my times afloat on cruise ships.

Sorry and all that, but there are times in one's life that funny stories just don't happen, and big ship cruising is one of those times. I've tried, on occasion, to spice up my life on board. Like whenever I'm asked by my fellow passengers to take a photo of them.

I usually position the lens to cut off their heads or their right arm or left leg. I do this on purpose. Unfortunately, with today's technological gadgets people can immediately review their photos to see what a mess I've made of their anniversary or birthday or honeymoon shot, and ask you to take another.

Back in the days of real cameras, with 35mm film and battery powered flash guns, I could take a spoof photo and not worry about being found out 'cos everyone had to wait for several days to have the photos developed by a chemist, and by that time I wouldn't be anywhere near the recipient to get castigated.

instrument stores so I had a key to this private place with a bunk and no windows.

The band had the pick of the girls on the cruise, constantly lining up to date them. Naturally, being the most handsome out of all the blokes in the band, I could show several of the girls how difficult a job it was to look after the instruments store with a bunk and no windows.

I think that this cruise was the one that permeated the boating bug in my veins and gave me a love of river and ocean cruising.

Cruise ships have absolutely everything one requires for a week or so of rest. What else is there to do but rest on these ships? You can't go anywhere until the ship docks in some foreign port, so you might as well relax and enjoy the cruise.

Most ships have several restaurants, a theatre, a cinema, a swimming pool, a gymnasium, a massage parlour, a doctor's surgery, shops, lots of shops, a casino, someone to make your bed and do your laundry and bring your drinks to you... Sheer decadence.

All this, however, comes at a price – usually several thousand dollars per person plus gratuities. It's worth it, nevertheless, just to lie back and be treated like royalty. Cruise ship companies really know how to treat people, and they make sure that the customer is always right.

So I don't really have any humorous anecdotes about my times afloat on cruise ships.

Sorry and all that, but there are times in one's life that funny stories just don't happen, and big ship cruising is one of those times. I've tried, on occasion, to spice up my life on board. Like whenever I'm asked by my fellow passengers to take a photo of them.

I usually position the lens to cut off their heads or their right arm or left leg. I do this on purpose. Unfortunately, with today's technological gadgets people can immediately review their photos to see what a mess I've made of their anniversary or birthday or honeymoon shot, and ask you to take another.

Back in the days of real cameras, with 35mm film and battery powered flash guns, I could take a spoof photo and not worry about being found out 'cos everyone had to wait for several days to have the photos developed by a chemist, and by that time I wouldn't be anywhere near the recipient to get castigated.

Mind you, I do enjoy a good photo bomb. That's where you get into someone else's photo and make a stupid face, or stick two fingers up or moon at them with your trousers halfway down your legs to expose your arse, but you have to do this covertly and unseen or they will just delete the photo and try again when you've gone.

I've managed to get my ugly mush on numerous wedding party photos, birthday celebration photos and dinners out photos just by being in the right place at the right time.

I've often chuckled to myself with the thought that the photo's recipient takes an in-depth look at his or her celebration photo and exclaims, "Who the hell's that!" when they see me, dressed in the wrong attire and grinning stupidly at the lens.

***

My wife and I once disembarked in Acapulco. Standing on the dockside was an armed policeman, rifle at the ready to kill anyone remotely suspicious. I thought this was a good opportunity to get a photo with an armed policeman and my wife together. We approached the guy and, being unable to speak the lingo, I pointed to my camera. He must have thought that I wanted him to take the photo but I ushered him to my wife's side and stood back to take the picture.

Nope. No good. Not a very good shot, especially as he wasn't smiling. He just stood there, all bland and uninterested. I motioned to him to put his arm around my wife's shoulder.

He looked horrified. Nooo! Not in his brief to pose for a photo with his arm around this Englishman's wife. He was supposed to be protecting the tourists leaving the ship.

I walked up to him and positioned his arm around my wife's shoulder. Oh boy! He looked really embarrassed in front of the hordes of holidaymakers spilling from the ship like lines of wildebeests on the Maasai Mara Game Reserve. His rifle hung limply from his other shoulder.

I bet he was praying that his boss didn't appear round the corner to catch him posing with this mad photographer's woman! As soon as he heard my camera's shutter click he smartly retrieved his arm, straightened his jacket and bowed his head to my wife in a respectful farewell. I shook his hand and he beamed a friendly smile, exposing rows of paper white teeth... Too late for the photo.

***

It seems that each time I went big ship cruising, my grown-up rogue gene had been inhibited in some way from causing any mayhem.

Perhaps the ships' crews had overawed it with their pampering and their 'customer is always right' philosophy. Who knows? Perhaps it just decided to take a rest while cruising with me. Who knows? But having said all that, organising a big ship cruise is sometimes not as straightforward as you might think.

In 2019 I booked and paid for a fifteen day cruise around Italy and the west coast of the Balkans for myself and my wife.

I booked on one of the most up-market cruise lines, with a luxurious cabin that came with a butler that would take my shoes off if I asked him. This was to be our fiftieth wedding anniversary cruise and I almost had to sell my house to pay for it!

The cruise was due to take place in 2020 but we all know what happened then, don't we?

Grown-up rogue genes everywhere had decided to dabble in world affairs by encouraging a most insidious virus to descend on the whole planet. Everything came to a standstill. Hospitals were inundated with masses of sick people hardly able to breath and gasping for oxygen. Some hospitals reached saturation point with absolutely no bed on any ward able to take any patient.

With flu-like symptoms, but infinitely worse, the populace were housebound by the government who ordered everyone to 'stay home, protect the NHS, save lives.' So, with almost every business in the UK closed because the government's 'lockdown' directive instructed everyone to 'work from home', my cruise was cancelled.

TV news desks showed pictures of cruise ships moored off some coast like a sad pod of beached whales, and businesses started to lay blame on the government for making them bankrupt. Consequently, the Chancellor of the Exchequer announced a couple of schemes whereby businesses were given vast sums of money to help them over the effects of the lockdown. Those schemes cost the taxpayer billions of pounds and provided the perfect conditions for fraud, and I really would like to know when (if?) this money will ever be paid back in its entirety!

Anyway, despite the Prime Minister declaring that "Nobody will be out-of-pocket" because of this turbulent situation, the cruise line flatly refused to refund the wad of money that I had given to them.

It's true that they at first offered a voucher that I could use for a future cruise but I didn't trust them to uphold their part of the bargain and I politely refused this offer and requested a full refund. Anyway, why should they keep the large sum I had paid, to invest in some off-shore bank and earn interest, when I could put my money to a better use?

It transpires that I was right not to trust these people because I later heard bad karma about cruise lines dishing out such vouchers, then increasing the cost of the cruise and making the poor saps who had accepted the vouchers pay the increase in costs. This kind of rip-off gets right up my nose but more of this in a later chapter.

The cruise line's refusal was final, as far as they were concerned anyway, but I was not going to let matters lie. I printed off all the contentious emails that had passed between the cruise line and myself over a period of about three months and sent this pile of correspondence to my credit card supplier.

Now, despite what you have heard about these guys I think they are first class chaps.

Admittedly, credit card interest charges are sky high but if you pay off your credit card bills on time you don't get charged any interest. If you've got a huge sum of interest to pay off it serves you right for spending money that you don't have. Again, more of this later.

Much to my delight, the credit card company repaid every penny I had forked out to the cruise line. No arguments, no hassle. Reimbursement in time for my next credit card statement in about two weeks' time. Well done, chaps! I can only assume that they would take the matter of their reimbursement up with the cruise line direct, but in the event it saved me from a whole load of arguments culminating in vast solicitor's fees to get my money back. I bet my grown-up rogue gene didn't see that one coming! The jury is out on how this bloody awful virus was first let loose on the human race and there have been many mutations in it since, all with the same effects of making people seriously ill! At the time of writing, in the UK something like ten million cases have been reported. That's just short of fifteen per cent of the population of Britain. I wonder how many unreported cases there have been.

I fear that the world of Covid will not settle down for quite some time yet. I'm sure, however, that there will be a day when this virus thins out and we will all consider it to be no more harmful than the common cold.

If you've never taken a cruise in your life you should. Even if it means taking out a second mortgage to pay for it. It's fun, it's relaxing, it's comfortable, it's a different way to see foreign parts and you'll nosh some excellent grub. I'm sure your own grown-up rogue gene will appreciate the holiday.

CHAPTER TWENTY SEVEN

Bill's Brush with the Law

Before I finish strolling through big boat cruising, let me stray off the holiday path for a moment to describe the time I almost got arrested for annoying an American cop.

My grown-up rogue gene took a really malicious swipe at me on this occasion.

If you've ever taken a holiday in Cuba or Jamaica or Haiti or Mexico you will have had to change flights somewhere on route from the UK. I've never had a direct flight to, or from, these places and I've always had to change at either Miami or Houston airports. Don't ask me why 'cos I don't know. I'm sure there are plenty of other airports to change flights.

Here's a warning for those of you who are considering a holiday for the first time in any of those sunny climes.

Miami and Houston are the worst possible places to change flights... In my opinion!

My only advice about these places is 'Don't book a holiday that necessitates a flight change at Miami or Houston to get to your destination.' That goes whether you are going to your holiday destination or whether you are going home. There's a good reason for these words of wisdom. I've done it several times and they're not journeys any sane person would make voluntarily.

The reason is that these airports are, or were when I last passed through them, probably too small to cater for the vast amount of travellers changing flights to and from the Caribbean Islands.

On the occasions I've had the pleasure of changing flights at either of these particular airports I found them to be time wasting, brain smashing frustrated queues of exhausted people at passport control desks trying to get their luggage, and themselves, on to the next flight that they have to board. They really were nightmare journeys, but unfortunately passenger aircraft had to converge at these hubs to offload millions of passengers so as to take on millions more for their onward journeys.

And these places are crawling with armed cops. Big, mean looking guys.

One stare from them and you are rooted to the spot wondering what you have done or what the cop is going to do. It's like being stared at by a Gorgon. A single eye contact and you're turned to stone!

Travel agents don't help, either, by booking flights that intersect at these airports. I've been to the Caribbean several times, each time changing at Miami, and frustration was in abundance with each visit.

On one occasion my wife and I were on our way to Cancun with a close friend of ours.

Our friend had booked this holiday direct with the hotel in Cancun and arranging the flights was my task.

I knew that our flight to Cancun from the UK changed at Houston airport.

So, after careful consideration of the long queues at most airports, I arranged our connecting flight from Houston to our final destination to be at least four hours after we had landed at Houston from the UK.

All the bookings went through without a hitch but my grown-up rogue gene decided to give us a helping hand.

As I had booked a relatively late flight from the UK, I had time to check my emails on the day of our departure. Low-and-behold, our carrier from Houston to Cancun had reduced the time of our connection at Houston to one hour. I felt the gut-wrench of something going wrong with this impromptu amendment to our flight plans but there was nothing I could do about it now. Our flight from the UK could not be changed.

After printing out the email, and hoping that Houston airport would be void of all other passengers except ourselves, we travelled to Gatwick and boarded our flight from the UK. It was a forlorn hope to think that our flight change would take place without any problems.

On arrival at Houston we couldn't get anywhere near a passport control desk. Thousands upon thousands of passengers all queued to join yet another queue somewhere up the line to board another aircraft. The passport control desks fought to stem this unrelenting flow of passengers trying to change flights to their next destination.

There was nothing for it but to join a queue, any queue, in the hopes that this queue would reduce in length rapidly enough for us to be able to dash to our next boarding gate in time to catch our onward flight.

No chance whatsoever. There was about as much chance of us catching our next flight to Cancun as there was of us being transported, Star Trek style, to our final destination hotel.

Now, sometimes an airport operative interrogates these queues by asking if there is "anyone on flight ABC 123 that needs to catch a connecting flight."

Those that show their hands are extracted and taken to a fast-track desk to continue their journey. Not at this airport. This airport was far from user friendly. We just had to wait our turn in a never ending snake of a queue until we could reach the passport control desk.

After half an hour I decided that I'd had enough. Our queue was still a couple of miles long and we had moved a total distance of about three yards. With families pushing buggies overflowing with kids and towing suitcases and lugging surf boards and scuba gear and beach balls and guitars and golf bags full of golf clubs, it would take until midnight for us to get to the front of the queue so I decided to try to find someone willing to help us catch our connecting flight.

Leaving my suitcase for my wife to manage, I extracted myself from the queue and looked around for anyone remotely resembling an airport helper. Nobody. I did, however, see a woman wearing an airport style uniform exiting from a door behind the vast network of queues. I headed through the throngs towards this door.

I didn't know it, but I was being watched!

I knocked on the door. No answer. I gingerly opened the door and poked my head inside. No-one there. Closing the door I saw several airport operatives in a huddle about ten to fifteen yards to my right. I'll tackle one of those people to help us catch our connecting flight. Just as I approached the huddle it dissipated into the crowd. They just took off in all directions and I had no chance to catch any of them. With a sigh of frustration I turned round and headed back to my queue.

I was still being watched!

You've seen the queues at airports or in the post office or in banks and theatres. They snake from side to side around barriers strategically placed to make the queue of people shuffle to the desk. That's why it always takes so long to get to the desk. People are crammed into as little a space as is possible.

I had to duck under several barriers to get anywhere near my wife and friend waiting patiently in their snake to get to the passport control desk. They still had another ten metres of snake to travel and I was still being watched, more suspiciously, with probing eyes!

Out of the corner of my eye to my left, where a leg of the snake turns to double back on itself, I saw a cop. Maybe he can help to fast-track us to our connecting flight.

This cop had watched me peel from the queue, knock on the door, poke my head inside the room, poke my head out of the room, close the door, approach a huddle of airport operatives then turn round, duck under several snake barriers and then approach himself.

Standing facing him I was just about to open my mouth when this guy asks, in a most aggressive way, "What are you doing wandering around the airport?"

"I'm trying to find someone to help me."

"You shouldn't be wandering around the airport. Get back in line."

"I was only looking for some help."

"That's not my problem. My problem is you, wandering around the airport."

This guy was really beginning to get up my nose with his 'wandering around the airport' rhetoric.

"Is there an office I can go to, to get help?"

"What kind of help?," with an exasperated sigh.

Looking at my watch I say, "I've got about ten minutes to catch a connecting flight and we're nowhere near getting processed in this queue," hoping he would take pity.

"That's not my problem. You'll just have to wait your turn. Now get back in line." Another aggressive refrain.

"Okay. I was only asking."

"I've told you... Get out of my face and get back in line," putting his hand on his gun!

I turned to 'get back in line' and this bad-tempered guy orders "Hey, you. Wait!" I turned back to face him.

"If I see you wandering around the airport again I'll arrest you!"

I didn't respond to this officious power-mad cop. I just smiled politely at him.

Just as I backed away to 'get back in line' I heard the guy ask me, "Have you ever wondered why you Brits have got a bad reputation?"

That did it. Two can play at this verbal ping-pong. I respond with "Have you ever wondered why you American cops have got a worse reputation than us Brits?"

"Get back in line before I arrest you!"

Inevitably, we missed our connection and we extracted ourselves from the queue to find a representative's desk associated with our flight carrier to Cancun. I could feel the cop's gaze drilling into the back of my head like a tunnel boring machine but I ignored the feeling and went about my search for someone to help us. As we had now missed our connection it didn't matter too much if this bad tempered cop arrested me.

Finding an appropriate desk I explained that we had missed our connection and we needed help getting another flight. Being told that, "The earliest flight to Cancun is tomorrow," didn't do my already frayed mood any good. I demanded to see the supervisor. The lady behind the desk was in no doubt that I meant business and she went to find someone who could pacify my rising anger.

The supervisor listened to my story, inspected my emails to verify that they had cocked up my flight plans and offered to provide a chit for a night's bed and breakfast in a hotel close by. We graciously accepted the offer and the supervisor confirmed our following day's flight number and time. We departed to find the hotel.

Out of the corner of my eye I noticed that the 'cop with an attitude' had followed us to this desk and was stood about twenty yards away, eyeing me menacingly. I ignored him.

Although we had, in effect, lost a full day of our holiday, the girls were, at least, grateful that we arrived in Cancun the following day with all our luggage... And without them having to visit me in some prison far from our holiday venue!

So, the moral of this tale is this; if you're ever tempted to ask a cop in Houston for some help... Don't! Just 'get back in line'.

CHAPTER TWENTY EIGHT

Bill's Surprise Cruise

January 2001

On one of my quinquennial internet cruise searches for our wedding anniversary, I found one that appealed to my sense of adventure. After researching the web site to make sure that it was legitimate, I booked a place for my wife and myself.

I decided to keep it quiet to surprise her. My grown-up rogue gene took this as an opportunity to surprise me.

The nature of the cruise necessitated some careful planning. There were several flight changes and overnight hotel stopovers to arrange separately, so the planning stage was quite complicated. Eventually, however, I was satisfied that all the i's had been dotted and that all the t's had been crossed, and I sat back to admire my hard work and reflect on my depleted bank balance.

I forgot to mention this cruise to my wife, 'S'.

As time went by, S decided to remind me that our thirty first wedding anniversary was due in April.

Assuring her that I had fully booked an appropriate holiday she asked, "Oh? Where are we going this year?"

"The usual, on a cruise."

"Okay, where?"

My previous silence on the subject intrigued her. Good. It will be a nice surprise. I'll go into more detail a little nearer the date.

"Er... we'll be cruising down the Colorado River."

"Great! Sounds fun."

"Yea, you'll enjoy it."

With that she went away to do some more vacuuming or whatever it is that women do during the day.

Several weeks went by and I saw her getting ready to go out. I had forgotten about our cruise for the time being. What's more to the point is that I had forgotten to clarify the nature of the cruise.

"Going anywhere nice?" I asked as she donned her coat to go out.

"Not really. I'm just going shopping for some holiday clothes."

Right at that particular time it didn't occur to me that I hadn't explained what the cruise was all about, and it didn't occur to her to ask. I suppose she just assumed it to be a run-of-the-mill cruise with tables for ten in a massive restaurant with five star food on the menu.

Hours later she returned to relieve the car boot of its numerous department store clothes bags which she dangled from the crooks of her elbows. I helped her with this awkward load by opening the house door for her. It's the least I could do. Mind you, I had to close the car boot...

Inside the house she plonked the hundreds of shopping bags on the floor and breathed a sigh of relief. With a look of inward trepidation I suddenly realised that I had not yet told her about our forthcoming cruise!

"What have you bought, then?" I asked with interest.

"Not a lot. Just some holiday clothes."

"Let's have a look, then?" I asked.

She took out what seemed to be an expensive dress and a fetching bikini. She could wear bikinis back in those days.

"Erm... I don't think you'll be needing those." Wait for it...

"What's wrong? We are going on a cruise, aren't we?"

"Well, yes but not the kind of cruise you think it is," slowly distancing myself towards a suitable exit.

"What are you trying to tell me?"

It's time to come clean and 'fess up.

"We're going white-water rafting... "

A pregnant pause while that particular statement sank in.

"What? White-water rafting...?"

A bigger pause as she sat down on the nearest dining chair and surveyed the collection of bags spread across the floor.

"White-water rafting, and I've just gone and spent a fortune on some new dinner dresses, new shoes, new underwear, new everything, and all I need is a pair of jeans and a sweatshirt?"

"Er... Yep."

"Why didn't you warn me?"

"I forgot," looking a bit foolish.

"Well I hope you don't forget to pay the credit card bill because I'm not taking this lot back. And you can just jolly-well find a time and a place for me to wear these clothes."

I did... I had to.

Several nights out at a few really posh restaurants to show off her dinner dresses, with overnight stays in a few posh hotels with a swimming pool to show off her bikinis.

Why did grown-up rogue gene make me forget to let her know about our cruise down the Colorado River?
More to the point, why didn't my grown-up rogue gene prod her grown-up rogue gene to ask about it earlier?

***

June 2001

After a torturous trip across the Atlantic Ocean, then immediately west across North America, our plane eventually landed at Las Vegas. Taking a taxi from the airport we finally arrived at the hotel I had booked, very tired and very hungry. After a buffet snack we went to bed and slept like logs.

After a peaceful night's sleep we woke the following morning rested and raring to go. Breakfast, then out for a bit of sight-seeing for the day. Looking back I'm amazed at how Las Vegas has changed since we were there. Tall sky-scrapers have sprung out of the ground like a garden of flower seeds that had just been watered.

Anyway, we spent the day looking round the streets and returned to the hotel to prepare for the next phase of our journey to the Colorado River. I mooched around the hotel's casino watching poker players squander their life savings and crowds of people feeding hungry slot machines with few prospects of getting anything in return. They seemed to enjoy throwing money away. S went up to the room to reorganise our clothing.

Instructions from the company providing our 'cruise' down the Colorado River asserted that we each take one rucksack only on our trip. This was understandable, in view of the limited space on the raft that would convey us down the river. Clothes packing, therefore, required careful consideration. We would need as much clothing as we could carry for one week, allowing for 'emergency' changes of stuff that got too wet, or too smelly.

I was okay with that 'cos I never changed my clothes at the best of times. I believed then, as I do today, that the only way to get value for money out of one's clothes was to "wear them to death." So back in those days one pair of underpants was all I ever needed for the week, but I took a spare just in case.

With my rucksack just half full I gallantly surrendered some space to S for her rucksack's overflow. As long as my stash of duty free cigars was kept dry, I was happy.

That night we were faced with a poser. What do we do with our suitcases, now only half full because our rucksacks were taking a load? With a bit of lateral thinking we squashed all our remaining clothes into the smaller of our suitcases and then put this inside the larger one. A good temporary fix.

I lugged this suitcase down to the reception desk. We didn't have wheels on our suitcases back then.

After checking and confirming that we would be returning to this very same hotel in one week's time – do you now see why my initial bookings were complicated? – I asked for some storage space for my suitcase. The hotel receptionist asked what we were doing in the intervening period but after explaining that we were going white-water rafting she understood and ordered one of the bellboys to take our suitcase to a storage room. She gave me a receipt for it and that's the last we would see of the suitcase until our return.

I hoped that S had packed my stash of duty-free cigars safely inside my rucksack 'cos there is nothing worse than having a cigar lighter with nothing to light.

The following morning we set off to find our next transport to the river. We must have looked like proper geeks. Ultra-clean clothes with razor sharp creases pressed into our Demins and shirts, new bright trainer shoes and hair neatly combed, with our rucksack on our backs.

Who cared what we looked like? We didn't. We were confident that we would look far worse than this on our return to the hotel.

Getting a taxi back to the airport we hunted round for someone carrying a placard displaying the name of our holiday host. Usually, these guys hang around the airport arrivals area but there was no-one of interest visible.

We were expecting a bus or a limousine or a taxi even, but what we found was something totally unexpected.

Thinking that perhaps our holiday rep was waiting for us outside we patrolled up and down the concourse looking for someone, anyone, carrying an appropriate sign. Out of the corner of my eye I caught sight of a chap with a placard on the ground floor of a multi-storey car park across the road from the airport arrivals door. Could he be the chap we were looking for?

Dodging the flowing traffic S and I dashed across the road and approached the guy who was proudly waving his piece of cardboard around as if he was on the stage of a huge auditorium. As soon as he saw us his face transformed into a friendly smile and he held out a welcoming hand to me.

After our introductions, and inspection of our paperwork, he bid us to follow him "to the plane".

Off he dashed, carrying our rucksacks, as S and I looked at each other in puzzlement. We weren't expecting another aircraft ride.

The guy ushered us to an open topped pickup truck and unceremoniously dumped our rucksacks in the back. We squashed into the cab and the guy drove out of the car park. He not only drove out of the car park, he drove out of Las Vegas! I was beginning to ask myself what I had let us into, or at least what my grown-up rogue gene had let us into!

After about twenty minutes of driving through the desert he pulled into a fenced-off area with a couple of low level aircraft hangars spread around a dusty runway. Driving up to a small single wing aircraft we emptied the pick-up truck and met another couple who had apparently arrived about ten minutes before S and myself.

Introductions over, the pilot stowed all our rucksacks into the belly of the plane, looked his passengers up and down, then instructed us, one-by-one, to board this matchbox toy of an aircraft. I was the last one told to board, and the pilot made me sit in the co-pilot's seat next to him "to balance the plane".

He joked about the fact that, "We won't get off the ground if you sit in the back."

Funny, eh? I wasn't all that stocky in those days. Strapped into the front seat I thought, "Fantastic! I'll get a good view of what we crash into."

Firing up the engine this tiny aircraft gathered speed as it laboured down the runway. Just as we almost arrived at the end of the runway the pilot pulled back on the stick and we were airborne. Everyone was excited as we climbed over the aircraft hangars and into the clouds as we all looked forward to the next phase of our adventure.

After about forty-five minutes we began our descent.

I don't know if the pilot usually descended in the manner that he did, but as we glided towards the ground the plane banked over to one side and swooped between a gap in the canyon side to emerge onto a large flood plain. We saw the Colorado River for the first time and the butterflies started to bounce up and down in everyone's stomach.

The plane bounced onto a makeshift runway and we all disembarked.

Collecting our rucksacks we loaded these onto a bus that took us to our hotel. After a night's sleep we all awoke to a hearty breakfast, a briefing and another bus ride to our rafts.

We were ready for the cruise of a lifetime down the Colorado River.

CHAPTER TWENTY NINE

Bill's Colorado Experience

White-water rafting down the Colorado River was great fun.

On two large inflatable rafts managed by two guys on each raft there were about two dozen tourists with all their rucksacks, all the food we would need for a week, tents, sleeping bags, cooking utensils, BBQs and a big rubber brick with the word 'Key' painted on it. What was that for?

The raft managers did everything. They steered the rafts through the rapids and along the river, moored up, unloaded the rafts, set up the cookhouse and cooked all the meals. Everything, at least for the first couple of days then we all mucked in with the unloading, setting up and re-loading the rafts.

As you can imagine, there are no toilets anywhere on the Colorado River so we had to have some rules about where to go and when. Here's where the big rubber brick with the word 'Key' painted on it comes into the picture.

Each time we moored up for the night one of the raft managers disappeared into some undergrowth with a spade. Making sure that the "toilet" area was sufficiently private he planted the spade in the sandy soil and came back out of the bushes, locating the big rubber brick at the entrance for all to see.

The system was that the brick was the "key" to the toilet. If it was visible the toilet was vacant. If the "key" was missing someone was at/on/in the toilet. Got it? The simplest solutions are always the best.

The trouble was, idiots kept absentmindedly leaving the key at/on/in the toilet when they had finished digging a hole [with the spade] and burying their 'sausages', so the rest of us were left 'holding on' to whatever we held on to, when we needed the toilet. Eventually someone would cotton on to the fact that the key had been left at/on/in the toilet and with an exasperated cry of "Who was the last one to use the key?" that person disappeared to relieve themselves of their load. Nobody ever answered that question so we never knew who kept leaving the key at/on/in the toilet.

Urinating was easy. You didn't need to dig a hole because the toilet was always positioned next to the river and the river took the brunt of our expelled booze. Actually, an alternative to urinating at/on/in the toilet was to hang on until you took a bath in the river in full view of everyone while wearing your swimming trunks. You could then pee to your heart's content without anyone knowing.

You had to have a strong will to take a bath, though, because the water was really cold... Except when you peed. I got so used to urinating in the river that when I returned to the UK I kept getting up in the middle of the night to pee into a pond that I had in our back garden! I didn't have any fish in this pond, but after a week I didn't have any frogs, either.

When darkness descended upon us we sat round a blazing campfire while one of the raft managers related stories to us about the history of the Grand Canyon and its various explorers and occupants.

For the first couple of nights we slept under the stars. Pure magic, although we had some reservations about sleeping out in the open when we woke to find our sleeping bags surrounded by large strange footprints! Our hosts, however, assured us that we were safe from meat eating animals. Now this begs the question, "Are there only vegetarian Mountain Cats in the Grand Canyon?"

The third night proved to be a proper nightmare. A howling gale descended on us and we had to shelter behind our rucksacks to keep our faces from being sanded down to the bone. After that night the hosts caved in to our pleas for a tent.

At the end of our cruise we were lifted out of the canyon in a helicopter and taken to a local restaurant for a shower and a meal. A small bus then transported us back to Las Vegas where my wife and I got a taxi to our previous hotel.

What a sight we must have made trundling into the hotel foyer with dusty clothes and bedraggled hair. We both got a lot of sideways looks by the clean, well shaved, well pressed punters on their way to losing all their life savings.

That white-water rafting holiday through the Grand Canyon was one of the best I've ever had. You should try it.

Unfortunately, my wife refuses to do it again.

CHAPTER THIRTY

Bill's Jest

Narrowboats. We've all seen them, I'm sure.

The vast majority of these crafts are pleasure boats, gently putt-putting along the waterway with wannabe ship captains standing proud on the rear deck. I've hired a few myself and I've even owned one. They're good fun and, with a speed of between three and five miles per hour, there is nothing to do but to take in the air and relax.

Do you want some boring history stuff on these boats? Okay, sit back and get ready to doze off.

With the onset of steam power, coal became the fuel of the times and required transporting from the coal pits and ports to various locations throughout the UK during the industrial revolution. Narrowboats were originally constructed to transport such goods along the network of canals dug by navvies (navigators) using nothing more than picks, shovels, wheelbarrows and hard manual labour. Once the channel had been dug out and the spoil carted away an army of 'puddlers' followed, on their knees with a bucket of water 'puddling' the clay with their hands to provide a watertight seal. The digging part was hard work, and a rota was agreed to give these men some rest by temporarily utilising them as puddlers until they had sufficiently rested before continuing to dig. As hard as the digging may have been I bet that puddling bored the men out of their minds!

I read somewhere that the navvies were Irish farm labourers who brought their families over to England to get away from the starvation caused by the potato famine. I'm not too sure about the veracity of that but English labour was, in any event, in short supply so I guess that the Irish navvies made up the numbers. I understand that narrow boats evolved as the canals were being dug and that the navvies and their families lived on the finished sections of canal in goods boats adapted to include living quarters.

However, in order to accommodate a boat in the narrow locks, constructed to convey boats from one river level to the next, the boats had to be less than seven feet wide and seventy five feet long, hence the term 'narrowboat'. Most narrowboats are six feet ten inches wide and the larger ones are seventy two feet long to provide some wriggle room inside the locks, although some locks will take a boat with a maximum length of fifty seven feet only because these locks were constructed shorter than others for some reason.

The original narrowboats were wooden crafts drawn by a horse walking on the canal towpath led by a crew member, often a child. The boats were chiefly designed for carrying cargo, although some packet boats carried passengers, luggage, mail and parcels and the first narrowboats certainly played a key part in the economic changes of the industrial revolution. But the arrival of the railways killed off the usefulness of commercial canal traffic and from about 1970 onwards narrowboats were converted into permanent residences or as holiday lettings.

Over a period of a few years I've boated on several of the waterways that criss-cross England and Wales; The River Thames, the Leeds and Liverpool canal, the Llangollen canal, Shropshire Union canal, The Cheshire ring, The Grand Union canal and the Oxford canal to name a few.

Okay, so now you know what a narrowboat is all about, let's get on with an annoying incident caused by my grown-up rogue gene during one of my holidays afloat.

***

I once took a boat over the Pennines. Yep, it's true. No, I didn't carry it over... I floated over the 'Backbone of Britain' via the Leeds & Liverpool Canal.

This waterway is a glorious voyage from start to finish, with breathtaking views, clean air to breathe and ninety one locks to negotiate. The canal rises to about two thousand five hundred feet above sea level, providing many opportunities for my grown-up rogue gene to strike.

Signing for the boat at Skipton we set off in the direction of Gargrave locks. The boatyard instructor travelled with us as far as the first lock to make sure I knew what I was doing. He would be picked up by his mate who drove the company van to meet him.

Arriving at the first lock I waited for the boat following us to catch up before closing the lock gates. Waving them forward I sat on the deck seat, resting my arms and chin on the tiller while watching the other boat approach.

I remember thinking that it was travelling a lot faster than it should, but perhaps the driver would slow down as it approached the lock.

Just to digress slightly, you should know that a golden rule of canal cruising is that you should never, ever, put your head, hands, arms, feet or legs outside the boat's gunwales unless you have tied up and are disembarking. There is a good chance that whatever appendage is dangling over the side of the boat will be shorn off if it gets trapped between another boat or against a lock wall.

Another thing to bear in mind is that one pays a sizable deposit to cover breakages on the boat prior to getting it signed over to you, so you have to make sure that you return the boat in the same condition as when you signed for it, which is usually pristine.

Anyway, I watched the other boat steaming towards us and thought to myself, "There's no way this guy is going to enter the lock at that speed without causing some serious damage to either his boat or to mine!"

With some reservation I could see this clown's boat heading straight into my stern – the rear of the boat – and I was determined that the impact would not cause any damage to us. I decided to fend off the speeding boat by pushing it sideways with my foot.

This decision was one of my more stupid ones!

Dangling my leg over the guard rail at the rear I waited to make contact with the oncoming boat's bow so as to push this to one side. At the time I was wearing a pair of comfortable running shoes but I doubt that any shoe would have been adequate enough to prevent what happened.

Diverting a two ton boat in full throttle coming at you head on is virtually impossible. Only an immovable object, like another boat, can stop its forward motion and I realised, too late, that my attempt to stop the boat was useless.

My foot got trapped between the other boat's bow and my guard rail. As the front of the bow slid across my trapped foot and trespassed into my deck space my foot was pushed sideways and I knew from the intense pain I was feeling that something was not quite right with it. It was clear that it had been crushed! My guard rail had buckled under the impact.

Fortunately the boat instructor witnessed this collision and he came to assure us that we would not be held responsible for any damage to our boat. After giving the other driver a severe reprimand, with lots of expletives and a red face in anger, he headed towards his mate with the van to take him home. I sent my son after him to bring him back to me.

On his return I asked him if he could take me to the nearest A&E hospital because I suspected that my foot would need some TLC. He not only took me and my son to the hospital, he stayed there until we were ready to be driven back to the boat. Good man!

My son helped me hobble into the A&E where a receptionist was waiting to take my details. After a short wait I was seen by the doctor. I was a bit miffed 'cos he cut through my laces to extract my foot from my shoe. I would have to buy a new pair of laces... He could have just undone the lace, couldn't he?

Anyway, after having an x-ray I took my x-ray films in a brown envelope back to A&E for some treatment. The doctor advised that four of the toes on my foot had been dislocated and that these would need to be relocated. He could do this, he told me, and bid me to lie on the couch while the nurse went to fetch a mask attached to a bottle of gas.

The gas had absolutely no effect on me despite about two minutes of breathing in the stuff. I asked the nurse if she had turned the gas tap on but she just gave me a exasperated look and pushed the mask tighter onto my face.

The doctor reappeared. He explained how he was going to relocate my toes... To cut a long story short he was going to grab hold of all four toes at once, pull them away from my foot and then push them all back into their respective sockets in one go.

"This won't hurt at all," he said and, "You won't feel a thing."

Now, I keep being given that refrain every time I go to the dentist but it's all lies, isn't it? It's blatantly obvious that dentists have never had a jab in the mouth to supposedly numb the pain, and it's equally obvious that this doctor has never had four toes dislocated.

The gas still had no effect on me and I mentioned this to the nurse. She pushed the mask a little harder against my cheeks. I looked at the doctor with some suspicion because my foot had now swelled to the size of a melon.

I asked if he had done this before.

"Of course," he replied. "Many times. "

The gas still had had no effect on me and I mentioned it, again, to the nurse. No response.

The doctor took hold of my foot with one hand, took hold of all four of my toes with the other and despite the fact that the gas still had had no effect on me, he tugged and then eased my toes back into their sockets.

The pain during this three second operation was excruciating because the gas had no effect on me, and in the seconds that it took to relocate my toes I had uncontrollably lashed out with my other foot and kicked the guy on the arm.

The doc then said to me, with just a hint of sarcasm, "The gas didn't work, did it? Oh well, it's all done now," as if that was any consolation for the pain my now throbbing foot was giving me.

I looked at the doctor, who must have been expecting a "Thank you" from me and said to him, as calmly as possible, "There's only one problem, doc... "

"Oh? What's that?"

With a touch of my own sarcasm I replied, "Wrong foot!"

Now, this guy originated from India. I know 'cos he had told me earlier. Watching his Asian skin turn a ghostly white was quite a sight. He literally turned as white as self-rising flour while scanning from one foot to the other. I suppose he could see all sorts of law suits heading in his direction. I sat there grinning.

The nurse placed a comforting hand on the doc's arm and said, "He's joking."

With that the doc gave me a disapproving look and left the room.

As the nurse fitted a surgical boot on my foot she told me that she had felt the doc flinch when I told him, "Wrong foot." She said it was the funniest thing that she had seen for a long time, but I doubt that the doctor thought it was funny.

My son and I were taken back to our boat by the chap still waiting in the van outside the A&E department.

I had to wear the boot for the whole of the holiday. On the day before we were due to hand the boat in, I phoned for a taxi to take me back to the hospital for a check-up. The same doctor inspected my foot and he was pleased that the swelling had gone down, but I had to continue to wear the boot for another two months.

It was just as well because I didn't have a lace to tie up my running shoe.

CHAPTER THIRTY ONE

Bill's Close Call in a Lock

Floating along at three miles per hour didn't give my rogue gene much wriggle room to cause trouble. At least not until I bought a narrowboat of my own.

The craft was a Sea Otter narrowboat, collected from Walton Marina. That first trip in my own boat gave me the opportunity to learn its foibles but, being new, it had few.

One thing this boat had that was not present on other narrowboats was a hard rubber buffer around the perimeter of the hull. A brilliant idea, I thought, because there is nothing more annoying than the clash of hard steel as two boats came together. Nudges and minor bashes were common, especially in locks, but the vast majority of these little bonks were just harmless jolts. The hard rubber buffer on my boat softened the impact and although there was a small jolt, there were none of the hard shocks associated with such collisions.

One problem I found, however, was that the projecting rubber buffer tended to hook onto the edge of the hardstanding concrete surrounding the lock. If you didn't keep the boat away from the side as it lowered into the lock, when the water was allowed to escape through the lock paddles, you found the boat rotating as the water receded.

During one trip my wife {S} managed the boat while I managed the lock. On this occasion S motored into a full lock and sat on the boat while the upstream lock paddles were closed by me. To prevent the boat from drifting inside the lock, I had looped the mooring rope around a near side bollard. S took up the slack in the rope and waited for the boat to lower with the water level.

As I walked to the downstream paddles to release the water a guy ran up the lock slope and proceeded to wind up the nearside paddle ratchet, macho-style... Really fast.

Now, this macho-style winding can be dangerous. If boats are not controlled they tend to be sucked towards the downstream lock gates really fast and they bash into the gates, sometimes causing damage to the gate or the boat. Also, the water rushes out of the lock paddles ultra-fast and creates a tidal wave downstream that upsets many boat owners.

Anyway, releasing the water seriously fast doesn't give one a chance to stop the water flow if there is a problem inside the lock. The ideal way to let water out of a lock is to open the paddles slowly, but the guy must have been in a hurry to bring his boat into the lock after mine had departed.

You see these guys regularly, running around the lock as if there was a time limit on the period that one spends inside it. It's as if they are in a race to see who gets from A to B the fastest. They run like maniacs from one end of the lock to the other, winding up the paddles macho-style to either let the water in or let the water out and on a nice day they sweat profusely in their haste to get the gates open and steam out of the lock under full revs. These guys usually charge along the canal at several hundred knots per minute, creating a wake behind them that sends moored boats into a frenzy of uncontrolled leaps that strain against their mooring pins. These selfish boaters really are ignorant sods.

So, the water rushed out of the lock that S was in. I had my back to the lock with my boat in it as I asked the guy to slow down. He just looked at me and then dashed back to his own boat, no doubt to speed into the lock before I've had a chance to let mine out. I didn't hear S shouting my name.

Watching the guy run down the bank towards his boat I wished him a happy and tiring journey with a wry smile that said, "This guy is going to have a big accident one day." My daydream still didn't alert me to S calling my name. Much as anticipated, I watched the guy release his mooring ropes from the towpath and begin to steam towards the lock.

I thought to myself, "I'm going to be as slow as I possibly can be to prevent this guy winning his race. It was at this point that I heard a panicked scream coming from inside the lock.

Turning round I saw S hanging on to the deck seat for dear life as the stern began to let water over its sides! The boat buffer had hooked onto the top of the lock side and the front of the boat pointed skyward in a mock picture of a rocket preparing to launch itself from the launch pad.

It was not yet vertical but it was pretty damn close.

I didn't have time to lower the gate paddles slowly, the proper way to lower these. I just unhooked the ratchet brake and let each paddle freefall down with a resounding bash as the paddles came to rest. I didn't have time for the niceties of lock management.

My intention was to run back to the upstream paddles to let water into the lock slowly to re-float the boat, but just as I dropped the second of the two gate paddles the boat dropped off its hook and landed in the water with a mighty splash.

The mechanics of what happened are a bit unclear. I think what might have happened was that the sudden halt of water flowing through the paddle openings created a miniscule dam of water at that end of the lock that was just enough to lift the boat up a fraction and release it from its hook.

Anyway, whatever the reason, my boat was now bobbing up and down in the lock on waves created by its return to a horizontal plane. Phew! I felt my heart pound against my chest as the adrenalin pumped into my veins.

I cursed my grown-up rogue gene for engineering a potential sinking and loss of the expensive boat and all its belongings. I was really worried about that.

Oh, and S...? She was okay as well.

CHAPTER THIRTY TWO

Bill's Fishing Trip

Okay, before I leave the subject of holidays here's an update on a wonderful fishing holiday I recently had.

I don't know why but when I got back home people kept asking if I'd had a good time, so I thought I would save you the task of asking me but not really being interested.

Be aware of the spoiler alerts – grown-up rogue gene was on the prowl.

I booked a lake-side cabin close to a place called Launceston, Devon. What should have been a three and a half hour journey from my place in Leighton Buzzard actually took five and a quarter hours because I had to pick up my granddaughter from Guildford.

We stopped on the way for a snack and a drink. Guess what? The roadside cafe didn't have any drink. No tea, no coffee, no bottled drink. All due to the effects of a transport strike not allowing deliveries... Apparently.

We all asked for a glass of water and the waitress went to the ladies toilet for one... A burst pipe in the kitchen. I declined the glass of water.

I thought, "Surely, my rogue gene has had enough fun by now?"

How wrong can one get?

I went to pay for the meal but couldn't find my wallet, so my wife paid. But where is the wallet?

I searched every pocket, rummaged through the suitcases, emptied the car but no wallet. Then my wife mentioned that she "might have seen it on the dining room table".

Think back... Loaded the car, went round the house checking windows, finished up at the exit door. Wife was already in the car waiting to depart, so hurry up and lock the front door.

That's it! My wallet is still on the dining table. Rotten ba****d grown-up rogue gene laughed at me all the way to my dry lunch but we've now travelled too far to go back for the wallet.

With no more problems we arrived at the fishing venue, thirsty but ready to unpack.

Spoiler alert!

I got the key to my cabin from reception and then had to walk for about ten minutes to it.

What's this? Oh no! The door key doesn't fit. It seems to be the wrong one from reception. After a few choice words appertaining to the intelligence of the receptionist, I had another ten minute walk back to the reception to get the right key.

Now, the receptionist is quite adamant that, "that is the correct key," but she offered to accompany me back to the cabin to help me unlock the door. Another ten minute walk and we arrive at the cabin.

I'm now feeling a bit jaded and tired. My wife and granddaughter were sitting on the suitcases waiting to get in but... "What do you mean, wrong cabin!"

"Cabin twelve is back the way we came. This is cabin twenty-one," advised the receptionist.

This time it's only a five minute hike lugging suitcases because the correct cabin is only half way back along the road to the reception. After a sheepish apology to the receptionist we're installed in the correct cabin and now ready to unpack.

I decide to go for a recce of the lake. However, I notice that this so called "lakeside" cabin is about a quarter hour hike through an assortment of brambles, rivers, ditches and muddy fields.

My shoes, the ones I intended to wear for our trips out to pubs, restaurants, sightseeing, and dancing, got really muddy and wet and ruined. I should have put my wellies on but I didn't bring them 'cos I didn't expect to have to yomp over tank tracks and a local rubbish tip. Well done, grown-up rogue gene.

My trousers have been torn by the brambles and I really ought to go to A&E to have these lacerations on my leg seen to.

On returning to the cabin I find a map hung up for all to see indicating a route of about one minute to the lake down a tarmac path at the back of the hut.

Ready to relax? Ha!

After a good night's sleep and a meagre breakfast of two eggs, four rashers of bacon, a lump of black pudding, five sausages, half a tin of beans, three fried tomatoes, three slices of toast, two more slices of toast, this time with marmalade, and two pints of coffee, and don't forget the pint glass of orange juice, it's time to go fishing.

Now there are a few rules that the lake owner has imposed. The most crucial is not to spread disease from one lake to another. So a rule enforced by the lake owner is that anglers must use the lake's own landing net unless the one you bring is a new one. This stops cross contamination of disease from one lake to another.

What's a landing net you ask? Well, the description is in the name. It's a net used to land fish that have been caught and reeled in. So, it's a large net that can be screwed onto a long pole so that one can reach the water. Okay?

Okay. Now, my description of a landing net is 'the net and the pole' because the net is utterly useless without the pole. So, knowing that the lake owner will supply a landing net I left mine at home.

Wrong move.

Before going down to the lake I went back to the reception hut to ask for a landing net. The guy brought out precisely that... A large net without a pole! I got a sinking feeling in the pit of my stomach suggesting that my rogue gene is grinning from ear-to-ear.

"Have you got a spare pole I can borrow?"

"Sorry, I don't keep spare poles but there is a shop in the local village that will sell you one."

Okay, think quick. I'll nip down to the shop to buy a pole so I'll take this net.

"That'll be twenty pounds for a deposit 'cos my landing nets keep being nicked," declares the bloke.

Great. My wallet is on the dining table at home two hundred and ninety miles away. Bloody grown-up rogue gene! I'll just nip back to the cabin (five minutes away) to tap my wife for the deposit. I trotted back to the cabin, then back to reception with my wife's credit card.

"Net, please."

"Oh, didn't I say... Cash only!"

I looked at this guy with just a hint of hatred on my face. Two hundred and ninety miles to a scenic lake with fish the size of whales to catch, and I can't go fishing!

Okay, think quick. If I've got to go buy a landing net pole then I may as well buy the whole lot – the net plus the pole. So I'll now have two landing nets but it never harms to have a spare. The lake owner can shove his incomplete landing net... Somewhere.

Tempus fugit, so I return to the cabin, another five minutes, to find that my wife and granddaughter have taken the car and gone to the same village that sells my landing net. I start to walk.

Another wrong move.

I've walked for about forty five minutes, that's about two and a quarter miles at three m.p.h., and there's no sign of a hamlet, town, city or even farm. Nothing but narrow tarmac, waist high bushes, fields and a cloudy sky... Ominous? And certainly no sign of my car with my wife and granddaughter.

I'm beginning to think about finding a place to sleep for the night when a tractor headed towards me. I don't actually flag this tractor down. I stand in the middle of the road to wait for it to stop 'cos I suspect this guy is going to keep going.

He slowed down and unexpectedly turned through an opening in the hedge about ten yards in front of me. I'm gob struck. I didn't see that coming, but I ran into the field that the tractor had turned into and eventually caught up with it.

I ask the driver, "How far is the town?"

"From here, about seven miles in that direction," says he, pointing back the way I've just come.

I've been walking in the wrong direction for forty five minutes? Bloody grown-up rogue gene does not want me to go fishing, does it?

So, another forty five minutes later I arrive back at the cabin. This sky is looking dark.

I've walked for about four and a half miles already and I've got another three to go. Then, with a bit of good fortune, my car returned. I looked at my watch. It's now almost lunch time so we decide to have a bite to eat.

After lunch I got in the car and set off for the town to buy my new landing net... And don't forget the pole! Don't worry, I've asked for directions which have been written down for me by my wife. I notice that evening gets earlier in this part of the country 'cos it's getting darker.

Phew! I found the fishing tackle shop without any problem and there is a place to park. Inside the shop I'm in a breath-taking Aladdin's cave of fishing equipment. It's like I'm six years old again and I'm scanning the inside of a sweet shop. I asked the bloke behind the counter for a landing net and behold, he produces exactly what I need. A net large enough for the biggest whale one could catch and a carbon fibre pole. Expensive but it will be my favourite, most used net, and my existing net will be my spare.

Yes, I'll take it. I reach for my wallet to pay for it...

I could repeat the choice words that I shouted at the guy behind the counter but they're not printable, so I let go of his neck and growled that I'll be back for the net shortly. I'm not sure if he was more relieved that I was returning with a wad of cash or, more likely, that I'd let him breathe again.

Back to the cabin for my wife's credit card. Those sooty looking clouds have slowed down and seem to be hovering above the town.

On returning to the shop I find that there is a new victim behind the counter. I asked where the first guy was, mainly because I really wanted to apologise for my earlier actions. You remember? When I lost it?

This new guy told me that the previous guy has been taken home because he's "in a state" after some madman had tried to throttle him earlier. I tried to look nonchalant, and purchased a new landing net.

Now I can go fishing, but it's almost two-thirty in the afternoon and it's getting a bit blustery.

Back at the cabin I decided to check my tackle bag to make sure I have everything I need for a few hours of peaceful fishing before tea and, not least, before that grown-up rogue gene takes another swipe at me.

Everything in good order. Here we go, then. With my tackle bag over my shoulder I picked up my chair, my new landing net, plus pole, and my brolly with my left hand and then bend down to pick up my bait bucket and rod with my right hand. A well-practiced tradition that always gets me to the bankside.

What rod? Where is it? I stand in the middle of the room looking round in case I've left it propped up in a corner. Nope. Not in this room. Is it still in the car? I unceremoniously dump everything on the floor and search the car. No luck. Do you think my grown-up rogue gene is toying with my emotions again? Think. When did you last see the rod?

When I was loading the car.

Okay, think laterally.

I telephone my neighbour to ask him to take a look in my conservatory. That's where I keep my rod.

Before I can ask the question I'm greeted with a cheery, "Hello Bill. I've just walked past your place and found your rod on the driveway, so I took it in to save it from being nicked. It looks like it's been run over."

Fortunately, absolutely nobody is in the room with me or they would have exited head first through the nearest window.

On my way back to the fishing shop it begins to spit with rain. Not much, but enough to be noticed by my automatic wipers.

With my new rod lounging on the back seat of the car, minus a hefty fifty-five pounds from my wife's credit card, I head back to the cabin. On arrival I load all my gear back onto my frame and head for the lake.

There is a huge crash and the sky is lit up like a Christmas tree with sheet lightning and I'm immediately drenched by what feels like a bucket of water. No, three buckets as it pours with rain.

I decided not to go fishing that day...

BOOK 4

THAT'S LIFE

I thought I would sweep up those residual memories that are lounging in my head. The ones that don't belong in any of the previous sections.

I had to wrestle with my deliberations, though, because I couldn't think of any specific section to put them in. So, after much contemplation I decided to let them languish in a section that looks at life in general.

I'm confident that many of you will relate to some of the scenarios that follow...

CHAPTER THIRTY THREE
Grumpy Old Bill

I don't know if anyone out there has noticed, but having to contend with a grown-up rogue gene for years and growing old at the same time changes a person.

I've become a grumpy old man but I bet you that I'm not the only one to experience such a change. There must be a few... Okay hundreds... All right, thousands of men like me who don't feel any different than they did when they were twenty-five years old but can, and will, find many things to complain about now. These things make life for grumpy old men purgatory.

Yes, I'm guilty of doing, or not doing, senior moment things like forgetting to zip up my trousers after I've just had a wee-wee or slopping gravy and food, mainly gravy, down the front of my t-shirt. I wear odd socks occasionally and fart just as I'm leaving the room to go to the toilet. Sometimes that fart turns out to be an explosion of an unexpected bout of watery diarrhoea! Yuk...

We've all done these things, haven't we?

Unfortunately we keep being reminded that we are grumpy old men by our wives, partners, children and anyone else who doesn't like something we've done or said or even just the way we've looked at them. I'm constantly reminded that "It's not what you do, it's the way you do it!" Personally, I can't see any difference in the way I "do" things than I did fifty years ago, but I suppose the difference is more noticeable as we age. The problem here is that the more I keep being told I am a grumpy old man, the grumpier I get 'cos I've just been reminded about it. It's typecast and it's a vicious circle.

In this chapter I thought I would try to relate some of the things that get right up my nose. You know, the things that make me grumpy enough to make my wife tell me I'm being grumpy. Let's start with clothes.

For some inexplicable reason, clothes manufacturers seem to have stopped putting labels on pullovers. How do they expect us oldies to put our pullovers on the right way round? The only way I know that my woolly pully is on back-to-front is when it strangles my Adam's apple. So, clothes manufacturers, please put labels on all pullovers.

Having said that, there is absolutely no excuse for me putting on my underpants and t-shirts back-to-front or even inside-out! Yes, there are labels on my underpants and t-shirts, but I sometimes miss them. Again, I don't notice this until my t-shirt garrottes me and it is downright uncomfortable with your pants on back-to-front. Only men know how uncomfortable that is!

Another penalty for growing old is that you tend to lose certain bodily functions.

Going deaf, for example. I've been gradually going deaf for years. I know it, but I flatly refuse to accept it.

My deafness began to be noticed by everyone whenever I turned the TV up a couple of notches because the actors constantly muttered. Why can't the TV Directors direct the actors to speak more clearly for people like me. Perhaps the Directors should also have words with the sound engineers to get them to pump up the volume a bit.

Here's something else that irritates both my wife and myself, and even the neighbours; I turn the TV up to be able to understand what's being said. My wife, and anyone else in the room, eventually acclimatises to the volume but then what happens? The programme cuts to an advertisement break and the noise from the adverts surprises everyone, even those passing by outside. So I turn the volume down... And then I can't hear what's being said when the programme returns and the actors start to mumble again. Infuriating, or what? The one button on my TV handset that always wears out first is the volume button.

However, I've found a solution to the problem of my deafness. I've purchased a wi-fi headset. The sound is great. As loud as I like and nobody complains. I can hear every word being muttered on the TV. This solution does, nonetheless, create problems of its own; when I've got the headset on I can hear the TV okay, but nothing else. Now, this irritates my wife because she talks to me and I don't reply 'cos I never heard her talk.

"Do you want a cup of tea?" is a good example.

No response.

"Bill, do you want a cup of tea?" a bit louder.

Still no response 'cos the volume on the headset is up high to overcome the effects of my tinnitus. So, because she's in a huff about me ignoring her, my wife gets up and goes to make a cup of tea just for herself.

When she returns, cup in hand, I make matters worse by asking "Didn't you make me one?"

Memory is another function that deteriorates with age, especially short term memory. I can remember events that happened years and years ago, hence my biographies, but can I remember my home telephone number or post code when I need them? Nope! I'll be laying in bed, just on the cusp of falling to sleep when the bloody telephone number comes back to me! Quite why I need it there and then is anybody's guess.

What about practical things like making the tea? I've lost count of the number of times I have put the t-bag in the cup but forgotten to turn the kettle on. It's a bit of a surprise when you expect a nice hot cup of tea but you get a cold drink instead. The Americans apparently like iced tea, don't they? I don't. And for some inexplicable reason I occasionally drop the t-bag into the water receptacle in the coffee machine. It's a hell of a job trying to fish the t-bag out.

Talking of coffee machines, how many times have you filled the water chamber, loaded the coffee granules and then forgotten to put the bloody jug on its hotplate under the granules cone water outlet? I do it a lot and it makes a right mess of the worktop as the coffee overflows the granules cone. I sometimes forget to fill the thing with water and turn it on, returning later to find nothing has happened!

Names are other bits of information that are sometimes useful. Can I remember a name when I need it? No chance. I once organised a reunion for my army pals. The reunion committee greeted everyone as they entered the dining hall. Could I remember the name of a close friend? His wife's name, yes, but his? It's a bit embarrassing when a close friend looks you in the eye and says, "It's me, Bill... {Name}," with a look of puzzlement on his face.

My eyes are failing and I have to get them closer to the book I'm reading to decipher the words from the blur, although my spectacles do help with this... If only I could find them!

My joints creak and crack, especially when I stand up and my once manly six-pack has sagged downwards and outwards. My six-pack has turned into a barrel!

There are several other bodily functions that have deteriorated or become slack, or even stopped working altogether, but I'll not go into those. I'm sure you get the message.

On the subject of health, Here's a gripe that I'm sure everyone in the UK has made; I've just tried to make an appointment to see a doctor. What a palaver!

When I first moved to my present abode one could phone up to see a doctor and get an appointment that afternoon. The local council, however, decided that a good way to increase their revenue was to approve the building of thousands of houses on some beautiful greenfield sites. I doubt that any thought was given to the infrastructure; roads, doctor's surgeries, schools, etc., because my quiet market town has been turned into a vast car park 'cos the roads cannot cope with the increased volume of traffic created by the explosion of estates that have sprung up on the outskirts of the town. The surgeries are so over-subscribed that the chances of getting a doctor's appointment this side of four weeks time is highly remote. In fact impossible!

I contracted Covid when it first descended upon the UK. I took to my bed and for three days and three nights I coughed my lungs inside out. I didn't eat or sleep for the whole of that period. When my temperature elevated to ceiling height and I started to gasp for air, my wife phoned the 111 number for advice. However, having explained to the operative on the other end of the line how I was in a bad way my wife was told to take me to a doctor. How the bloody hell could I have made it to a doctor in the semi-conscious state I was in? But as far as the 111 operative was concerned it "... just sounds like he's got the flu."

It wasn't very long after this telephone call that the hospitals were inundated with Covid patients queueing up in corridors to wait for some treatment and a few litres of oxygen. So much for telephone help lines...

Oh, yes! Telephone help lines make me fume. One has to negotiate about ten different menus only to be told to telephone a different help line number because the one that has just put you on hold for about thirty minutes... Sometimes longer, is the wrong department to help with your query.

And do not get me started on telephone marketing! They are an intrusion and they are a bloody nuisance. I usually ask the marketeer from India to explain what they want, in the greatest of detail possible, then lay the phone down to let these guys talk to themselves and waste their client's money on a call that nobody is listening to. If they are still on the line when I pick the phone up in five minutes time I just cut them off.

Here's a good one. Can anybody tell me why my dentist charges me for work? Dental practices make great play on the fact that they are an NHS dentist, yet they charge me an arm and a leg to have a filling. I have to take out a second mortgage to have a tooth crowned. Even a simple inspection costs me. I always understood the NHS to be free of charge when one gets to my age, so what do my hard earned taxes pay for? What have I worked for, all those years, and where have the taxes I have paid gone?

Oh Boy! Where's my soap box?

That's another thing I beef about... Taxes. I've worked hard all my life, I've paid every penny of the taxes that the government has demanded and compulsorily extracted from me. I've worked and saved and worked and saved, just so that I can live a comfortable life for the rest of my life, and now, when I've got only my hard earned pensions to live on, the government claws more money back from me with the excuse that I must pay income tax on my pensions. They don't miss a trick, do they?

In the meantime, some greedy avaricious politician uses my taxes to pay for a duck house for the pond at the bottom of his vast garden, while another politician uses more of my taxes to redecorate his home. Yet another politician will claim the rent he has to pay for his palatial London flat from my taxes while he derives a huge income from the rent he is charging for an abode a couple of streets away. They will tell you that this is not wrong... It is allowed under the rules that they, themselves, have made! Greedy pigs.

One thing that really annoys me is the 'cancel culture' that we Brits have accepted as the norm.

I read in the newspaper this morning that a woman who is the wife of a brother of a nephew of some bloke that is an uncle to the sister of another bloke who picked his nose in the 1700s had had her prominent statue taken down because the bloke who picked his nose was related in some way to another bloke who was loosely connected to the slave trade. The slave trade was stopped years and years ago. Long before any of us were born. We're not interested any more and anyway, you just cannot cancel history by badmouthing some poor unfortunate that just happens to be an ancestor of someone who did something that you don't like. I'm not saying that the slave trade was right. It wasn't. It was crass elitism intended to make rich people richer. What I'm saying is "Get over it!" All you 'do-gooders' should get a life and move on.

In my opinion there are too many do-gooding busy-bodies in this world and we would be a lot more tolerant if we just 'live and let live.'

I get grumpy at the argumentative and foul responses to social media posts that malign a person or complain about the colour of someone's eyes or whatever it is that people do to make a person feel insignificant. My answer to that is, "If you didn't use social media in the first place, you wouldn't see any obscene tweets." Who, in their right mind, would post a nude picture of themselves or tweet their every move or disclose every aspect of their very private conversations for all to see? You get what you deserve, you idiots, because by using these platforms you are making complete prats of yourselves. Right now, people are using social media to intimidate and extort money from innocents just like you, and people have committed suicide over the toxic posts about them! It's all wrong.

Newspapers and news channels... Don't even mention these media sources to me! It never ceases to amaze me how biased these outlets are. I understand that the BBC's motto is "Nation shall speak peace unto Nation." One puzzles at the biased way in which many of the BBC's news reports are presented to viewers, and I question if such bias reflects the BBC's intent to "... speak peace." Newspapers don't do much to present unbiased reports, either, when one measures the way in which people's credulity is stretched to its limit.

Next, I'm fed up with people sliding their greedy sweaty palms into my back pocket to grab as much money as they can for the dismal service that they provide. Restaurants, for example, charge a lot for a decent meal. Then they add a service charge on top of the wedge that you must find for the meal...

And the waiters/waitresses then look peeved if you don't give them a cash tip. What the hell is the service charge for? I guess that that goes straight into the fat-cat restaurant owner's wallet. Everybody is at it. Tradesmen, food providers, repair engineers, mechanics, restaurants, shops; anywhere and everywhere a service is provided. Anywhere you have to pay for something. I agree with the principle of making a profit. After all, without a profit a business cannot survive. But when businesses charge exorbitant rates for doing something that takes just a few minutes that gets right up my nose.

And I firmly believe that 'money is the root of all evil'. Greed seems to dictate every sinew of our lives. One day, say Monday, everyone is happy – Suppliers, consumers, manufacturers, service providers, etc. Then suddenly on the very next day, Tuesday, everything has to have a price increase. Why? If everyone is happy with what they get on a particular day, why does one greedy pig have to upset the equilibrium by demanding more on the following day? When you ask 'A' why he/she was satisfied on Monday but wants more on Tuesday, 'A' will pass the excuse up the line to 'B', who will pass the excuse up the line to 'C', and on it goes. We ask the same question on every price change and we get the same answer... Inflation. Why inflate the price of things if you already make a tidy profit? Because – it – provides – a – bigger – profit! We must be muppets for going along with it.

I bet you that lots of pensioners out there will relate to this last gripe.

I'm slowly turning into an exact copy of my dad! Honest. A mirror image in terms of looks, attitudes, outlook on life, tolerance, dress code, the lot. Absolutely everything! Don't get me wrong with this. I loved both my parents dearly and was devastated when they died. But all the things about my dad that I made fun of seem to be descending on me with a vengeance.

When he was in a fit working state he had a bad accident. He was at the top of a thirty foot ladder inside a school assembly hall repairing the roof. At that time ladders didn't have anti-slip feet, just plain wood. Always one for 'safety first' dad insisted on taking another guy with him to stabilise the ladder and prevent this from sliding while he was on it. Everything went to plan until the safety guy 'footing' the bottom of the ladder to stop it sliding decided to walk away from it. Yep, the ladder's feet decided to follow the bloke and dad followed the ladder down to its horizontal resting place on the hard parquet floor. Dad got a crushed hip, broken jaw, a displaced vertebrae in his neck, broken ribs and a bump on the head that put him into a coma for over a week. I was given compassionate leave from the army to be with him. The result of this accident was that dad never went back to work following his recovery. He couldn't. He was unable to climb ladders and no climbing ladders meant no job.

Whilst in a coma the surgeon elected to give him a hip replacement operation, and in later years he developed the painful neck related condition Cervical Spondylosis. His rogue gene really went to town! However, I have fond memories of joking with dad about his walking stick and the times he chased my brothers and I for mickey-taking his stiff neck, his head held upright by a neck brace.

Anyway, my grown-up rogue gene has now decided to punish me for all that mickey-taking. I've now developed a stiff and painful neck and my hip locks into place if I sit in the wrong position or stand for too long or walk long distances. My nose has expanded in several directions and I continually grow embarrassing unwanted hair that has to be trimmed from my nose, ears and eyebrows. It really is no joke getting old.

Frankly, all the things I've mentioned in this chapter really do add up to make a person grumpy, and the more one gets grumpy with such things the grumpier one gets.

***

Is there an answer to all this? Yes! There is. I've started to talk to things.

I say to my right leg, "C'mon leg, get in the car," as I lift it over the sill and into the footwell. I talk to socks and pants and trousers and cupboards and drawers and garage tools and chairs and light bulbs... In fact anything that doesn't answer back. I have quite a lot of intelligent conversations with my PC and its accessories and, indeed, with myself! Why is that? I don't know.

I talk more to inanimate objects, and that includes me, than I do to my wife! Perhaps it's because inanimate objects can't disagree with me. I may have mentioned to you at some stage that Yorkshire men are never wrong. I don't know whether I have mentioned this before because my memory is fading... I've now even forgotten what this chapter is about!

Oh, yes... Grumpy old Bill.

What I do know is that it helps to call the kettle a pillock, or blame the front door when I have just locked myself out. It helps by reminding me not to be such a grumpy old man and it prods me to being more tolerant. It also reminds my grown-up rogue gene that there is still some fight left in me!

"There's only one certain thing in life, and that's death," as the maxim goes. That's true, but if you have any sense at all you will heed my warning that you will undoubtedly grow old and grumpy before you die.

CHAPTER THIRTY FOUR

Bill's Technology

Okay, enough moaning. Can we take a brief look at technology?

Albert Einstein, the German-born theoretical physicist who developed the theory of relativity, once stated, "I fear the day when technology overlaps with our humanity. The world will only have a generation of idiots."

In my opinion he has been proved to be right. For example, look at the brain dead idiots focused on their mobile phones as they step off the pavement in front of a few tons of speeding metal that's guaranteed to cause severe damage to the idiot! In most cases they don't continue to be just brain damaged, the impact renders their whole body and soul inoperative... Dead! Not to worry, though, 'cos their mobile phones are designed to withstand harsh treatment. The phone will be infinitely more functional than the idiots' bodies or brains 'cos bodies or brains don't function very well splattered across the front of a bus.

Anyway, one day there will be no shops. You won't be able to 'nip out' to buy something quick. You won't be able to squeeze that orange to see how ripe it is. You won't be able to bounce up and down on that mattress to see how comfortable it is, or measure that sofa to see if it fits in that gap in the lounge. You won't need to go to the bank or Post Office. Forget going out for a take-away. Even going to church will be obsolete.

Why? Because everything, and I mean everything, we do to exist like buy food, clothes, commodities, presents, etc., will all be done on-line. Well, not literally everything. I can't make mad passionate love to my wife on-line, for example. At my age I can't make mad passionate love! But I think you get my drift.

Now, this futuristic existence will create an abundance of opportunities for grown-up rogue genes everywhere to flourish and cause a cornucopia of chaos. Let's face it, we already have problems with slow internet, no internet, hacked internet, and a whole new internet language that only kids in primary school can understand.

People give out their most intimate details to on-line places such as Facebook or Snapchat or Twitter or Instagram and a whole load more social media platforms. Gullible 'friends' have been persuaded to post photos of themselves, sometimes really intimate photos, on social media platforms which have then been used to shame, humiliate and demean the unfortunate subject of the photo. These platforms are even used for political gain!

If you choose to buy a product on-line you may have to 'register' with the supplier, although some suppliers allow you to order goods on-line as a 'Guest'. Nonetheless, out of necessity, when purchasing something online you need to provide your name, address, credit card details, sometimes your telephone number and the colour of your underpants! That last snippet of information doesn't sound as ridiculous as you may, at first, think. Order a pair of underpants on-line and what's one of the first things they ask? What colour do you want? All this information can be, and in many cases has been, hacked by fraudsters eager to relieve you of your hard-earned cash.

I'm told that today's privacy laws make it extremely difficult for suppliers to use your personal information covertly. Crooked hackers and, indeed, some suppliers have, however, still found ways to circumnavigate the law.

I accept that the 'Big Brother' scenario is a creation written by George Orwell in his dystopian 1949 novel entitled '1984'. He had mega foresight! Right now, 2022, the 'Big Brother' scenario is not such a myth as we imagine it to be.

As long ago as the late 1990s I was listening to news reports on the TV about emails being 'monitored' to prevent terrorist attacks. But you don't necessarily have to be on the internet to be 'monitored'. There is an army of CCTV (closed circuit television) cameras spread around the streets. Another name for CCTV is video surveillance and some of these cameras record precisely where you are travelling in your car, the speed that your vehicle is travelling and they also take a close-up mug shot of whoever is driving.

There are CCTV cameras on the sides of shops, inside shops, on the sides of homes, inside homes, inside and outside business premises, in car parks, outside supermarkets, inside supermarkets and many, many other locations to interlope into one's life.

Someone, somewhere, wants to watch you and watch what you are doing!

***

Let me tell you about the time I had an interesting conversation with one of the 'men in black'.

Yep, It's true! These men really exist. A real operative from a secret organisation telephoned me to give me what can only be described as a telephonic grilling...

When my grandson was knee high to a gnat in the early 2000s, like most boys of his age he went through a phase of wanting anything 'Transformers'. There was a new Transformer out that was "Really cool".

This was a toy truck and the wheels on this thing went round-and-round, just like the wheels on the bus...

Through a process of bending, folding, twisting and banging on the floor the truck transformed into a menacing robot with a missile launcher. With it you got several small missiles to launch, for free, but you soon ran out of these because the dog ate them, or they got sucked up into the vaccy cleaner, or they just got stood on and broke. Sometimes they got lost down the back of the settee or would end up stuck in your little sister's ear, or up her nose or even chewed to death by baby brother. These missiles were lethal when they were launched 'cos they could easily take out an eye!

Now, normally I would have gone to somewhere like Argos and bought one of these boys' toys. But we were, at that time, just in the infancy of on-line places like eBay (founded in 1995). Even email was a relatively new concept.

So I searched for 'Transformers' on eBay because I suspected I could get it cheaper than the shops and, in any event, would save me the trouble of going to the shops. Up popped a long list of Transformer toys and accessories and eventually I found the very same toy that my grandson had expressed a desire to own. Fantastic! But don't celebrate too soon, 'cos my grown-up rogue gene has just dragged himself out of bed.

 A couple of weeks after placing the order the postman drove up in his big red van, rummaged in the back and knocked on our door. He put this massive parcel on the ground in front of me asked me to 'Sign in the box', then thrust this brick sized gadget at me with a screen that was about two inches across. He gave me a stick-like thing about as long as a matchstick attached to the gadget with a curly lead that got in the way to sign with. No way was this thing going to represent a true illustration of my signature, so I put an 'X' in the box and gave the gadget back to the postman. He left without looking at what I had written.

I decided to check out this huge parcel and on opening it I found a mass of those nugget sized fragments that suddenly jump out and float all over the table and down to your carpet. Do you know that you can sometimes eat those bits of packing? Yep, it's true. They're made of rice paper which is edible, but I wouldn't advise cooking them in the oven first... Makes a right mess. And DO NOT eat too many. One'll be enough to put you off trying any more. They're a bit bland and chewy and they tend to bung up your insides.

So anyway, after stirring through this box of packing and scattering the bits around the table and carpet I found another box, this time about one-seventieth the size of the outer box. I'm sure they pack items in this ratio because they can't, or don't want to, dispose of the big boxes. Extracting the Transformer's box proved to be even more disruptive and messy than searching for it, with about seventy per cent of the edible packing being distributed around the room.

Spoiler alert! There are no missiles! "Hellooo, grown-up rogue gene."

I took both boxes apart to look for the missiles, spreading a lot more edible packing around the room, but the missiles were definitely absent. I cursed my grown-up rogue gene under my breath and got all the paperwork associated with this transaction in front of me. Ahh! An email address for the sender. I sent him an email explaining the absence of the missiles and asked if he could provide them for me.

I'm going from memory but my message went something like...

"Hi. Thank you for your prompt response to my order. I can confirm safe receipt of the Transformer. Unfortunately the missiles that were advertised with the consignment do not appear to have been placed in the box with the rest of the merchandise. Is there a possibility that these have been inadvertently omitted from the parcel? If so, can you please send the missiles to me as I would like to present the complete item as a gift. I look forward to your advice on this matter and will be happy to answer any queries that you may have."

An innocent request? No! My rogue gene was all over this like a rash and, I kid you not, within thirty minutes the telephone rang...

Me – "Hello, Bill Pollard."

A N Other – "Mr Pollard?"

"Yes, that's what I said. Who's calling?"

"Well, you don't know me but I've been instructed to telephone you about your recent enquiry for a missile."

I was loath to giving any information out without knowing who was telephoning me.

"What? What missile?"

"Have you requested a missile from someone?"

"When? What's your telephone number?" In those days telephones didn't have a caller number displayed.

"Doesn't matter. Are you looking for a missile?"

"What are you talking about?"

"The missile you've just requested via email to {the supplier's name}."

After a brief thought, "What's it got to do with you?"

"A lot."

"Who is this?" I indignantly questioned.

"Doesn't matter. Have you just asked for a missile to be sent to you?"

"Yes... No! Not a real one."

"Not a real one?"

"That's right, a toy missile."

"But a missile, nonetheless."

"What? What's your name?"

"Just call me James."

"Okay... James, What's the name of your company?"

"Doesn't matter. Are you able to prove it's a toy missile?"

"How did you get my phone number?"

"No... Doesn't matter."

Again, "What's your telephone number?"

"Doesn't matter. I'll ask you one more time. Are you looking for a missile?"

"Look!... Hang on, how do you know I've just been on the internet?"

"You don't need to know that. What missile are you trying to buy?"

"I don't have to answer these questions. I'm going to put the phone down."

"I wouldn't do that. It'll mean a visit to you and we're trying to watch expenditure."

"What?... I don't give a toss about your expenditure. If you want me to prove it's a toy missile, come round and play with it with my grandson. You could even pretend you're one of the Men In Black... "

I put the phone back onto its cradle and muttered, under my breath, some choice words about Big Brother and my grown-up rogue gene. I told my wife about this insane conversation and we were both gob struck.

I never heard from James again.

The missing [toy] missiles were posted to me, and they arrived safely and, indeed, well packed in a box ten times the size that was required.

***

There are many other technological gadgets that we have come to rely on.

Take sat-navs, for instance. There was a time when these things were just car accessories. Now, however, if you have a mobile phone with a big screen that you can swipe with your index finger you can install an 'app' that will show you where to go, where you've just come from and precisely where you are at any given time in your life. I can't do this because my mobile phone is so ancient that it should be in a museum. It still works, though.

Mind you, mobile phones have evolved quite briskly, haven't they? I remember a time when only busy executives had a mobile phone 'cos the only way to get one was via the company's expenses budget which just about covered the cost. It was a stretch to call these things 'mobile' phones.

They were lumps of plastic in the shape and size of a house brick and they were just about as heavy. They had a big rubber earpiece on one side resembling half a headset and a keypad with just the numbers nought to nine, together with a retractable aerial pointing skyward just waiting to poke someone's eye out. They resembled army communication radios you sometimes see in war films. A person could dial out, and a person could dial in. That's all.

Anyway, I digress.

Sat-navs are now integral with car dashboards but you can't carry your car can you? So you buy a phone that you can have poking out of your Demin jeans back pocket. Safe, or what? Still, you don't need a big paper map to show you the way. Do you remember those cumbersome paper maps? Can anyone say that they have been able to actually fold one of those expansive wallpaper sized sheets back into its original shape? I haven't. I went out and bought a book of maps so that I didn't have to do any map folding ever again.

There. I've done it again, haven't I? Departed from my original chain of thought...

The only problem with sat-navs, in general, is that the technology depends on math-based programs that require updating frequently, or your gadget doesn't know about the new bypass that you can take to cut about three hours from your journey. And another thing... We're so reliant on these things that we religiously believe them to be one hundred per cent spot-on. How many of you have driven down a narrow country lane to be confronted by a huge juggernaut heading towards you because his sat-nav told him to squeeze his huge articulated truck into this inappropriate thoroughfare?

Having said all that, I remember a time when I once hired a car in Cyprus so that my wife and I could visit plenty of touristy sights. The car came accompanied with a paper map. Deciding on an appropriate route to go visit the Troodos mountain region we set off.

Now, what you should know is that the car we had hired was a small one. Almost a Corgi toy, but we didn't need a big gas guzzling four-by-four 'cos this toy-sized car was a lot cheaper to feed, and we just had the two of us to do the exploring.

Relying on our map we drove up country. The roads, however, became narrower and narrower. We were soon driving on a narrow footpath sized dirt track with the paint on the car doors gradually being scraped off by the unyielding bushes closing in on us. The track was also getting to be a bit bumpy but the map informed us that this so called 'road' was a 'C' class road which, by all accounts, was supposed to be a good road, according to the guy that signed the car over to me.

We soon found out what a 'D' class road was like.

We had been advised by our car hirer not to take this class of road because it was unsuitable for cars, unless the vehicle was one of the four-wheel drive models. But our Corgi sized car definitely was not a four-wheel drive model.

We pressed on. It felt like we had driven onto a riverbed. The car bumped up and down on boulders that scraped the bottom of the car's oil sump at the front and the boot floor at the rear. The car's suspension springs were probably given the most demanding work-out they had ever experienced!

After about twenty minutes I was beginning to get a bit nervous about this particular route but we had, by that time, gone too far to turn round. We couldn't turn round anyway because the barrier of bushes either side of the car prevented us. To get off this river bed we would need to reverse back up the track, but I doubted that we would make it back to the road we left about twenty minutes ago without getting the car's rear end hooked up on a boulder.

After what seemed like a lifetime of bouncing, scraping, crunching and revving we suddenly emerged onto a better dust track. With a sigh of relief I parked up to take a rest. The concentration of driving along the riverbed had been immense.

Continuing our journey, once more, we suddenly came to a dead-end. Not just any dead-end but someone's house, and the occupants were having a party out on the patio that we had just driven onto.

Talk about looking surprised... The host approached us with arms waving and shouting profanities that we couldn't understand, anyway, because we couldn't speak any Greek. I apologised profusely and the host allowed us to turn round and return down his driveway. We didn't turn back onto the riverbed but carried on until we found an 'A' class road to continue our journey.

So what's the moral of this whole chapter? Well, don't get too reliant on the technology available to you whether this is the Internet, a car sat-nav, a mobile telephone or a paper map. If you do, your grown-up rogue gene will definitely enjoy upsetting your day.

CHAPTER THIRTY FIVE

Bill's Health

I was once briefly introduced to narcolepsy. I don't know why but I guess my grown-up rogue gene had decided to experiment for a while.

People with narcolepsy fall asleep without warning. Anywhere, anytime. You could be working or talking or you could be up a ladder or just eating your dinner. You are suddenly overcome with an unexpected sleepiness that forces your eyelids to close and persuades your brain to shut down for a while. When you wake up you feel refreshed, but you soon get sleepy once more. Strange, or what?

My dose of narcolepsy descended upon me when I was in the army. It's not the best of times to get afflicted because one is always marching or shooting or bulling one's kit, but my grown-up rogue gene decided to experiment and have some fun in the process.

I would be sat in the band room enjoying a bit of full band practice when suddenly I would be woken up by my mate sat next to me. It wasn't the first time. In fact, it wasn't the second or even third time! The Bandmaster (BM) would be stood there, staring at me with an annoyed face as the rest of the band all turned to look in my direction. Now, when you are the first trombone player in an army band falling asleep during rehearsals was not helpful, especially when you are striving for promotion. The BM ordered me into his office for a chat.

"Have you been drinking, Pollard?"

"At this time of the day? No sir."

"Were you out late last night?"

"No sir."

"Are you taking any drugs?"

"Absolutely not, sir."

"Well you had better get yourself up to the M.O. to find out what the hell is wrong with you because you're no good to me asleep."

On the way up to the medical centre I had visions of my place in the band, as top trombone player, being taken away from me.

It wasn't the correct time of the day to go sick. That's usually at eight a.m. so the medical centre was quiet. I knocked on the M.O's door and was bid inside and offered a chair next to the M.O's desk.

"What's the problem, Pollard?"

"The BM has ordered me to see you, sir."

"Okay, what's the problem?"

"Well, it's a bit embarrassing, sir."

"Okay, I'm a doctor. You can tell me. I won't say anything, honest."

"I keep falling asleep, sir."

"Yea, I know how you feel. I often fancy a kip during mess night," with a sarcastic smile.

"No, you've got it wrong, sir. I keep falling asleep at odd times."

"Oh? Like when?"

I explained.

The M.O. looked a bit puzzled and reached for his stethoscope and blood pressure monitor. He gave me a full medical examination. Absolutely everything. Heart, lungs, eyes, ears, nose, throat and lots of poking and prodding in lots of places. The M.O. then says to me, "Wait there while I go get a thermometer," and he left me sat in this really comfortable chair as he left this really quiet room.

The next thing I remember is being shaken by the M.O. He had been gone for a mere fifteen seconds but I was away, in the land of closed eyelids and relaxed brain. If he didn't believe what I had told him before, he certainly believed it now!

The M.O. sent me up to the military hospital, about ten minutes walk away. When I got there I handed in my letter from the M.O. and was ushered to a vacant cubicle. Once more I was given a full medical exam, this time with the addition of an EEG (Electroencephalogram). That's when they attach loads of wires to your head with small suckers and run a test that detects abnormalities in your brain waves. The hospital doctor was looking for the electrical activity of my brain. I know some blokes whose

EEG will register as a flat line even though they are awake and functioning.

They found nothing wrong, neurologically or physiologically, so they sent me back to the Battalion M.O. with a note requesting him to stop wasting their time.

For some inexplicable reason I was never troubled with narcolepsy again. I have absolutely no idea why, at that precise time in my life, this stupid complaint decided to descend upon me, to make me and the M.O. look like prats, but I've never forgotten the time I went sick to complain about falling asleep, then fell asleep while the Doc went to fetch a thermometer.

Back then, my grown-up rogue gene really knew how to embarrass people.

**

I once died.

It's true! Honestly. Absolutely no heart beat! Relax and I'll explain.

In 1972 my Battalion occupied Mons Barracks, Aldershot. During that summer the band performed in a variety of concerts, carnivals and Officer's Mess functions.

Now, holding a trombone in the correct position to make it sing takes a lot of practice and a good slide technique. The success of slide control is in the wrist and elbow action. You have to imagine that both your wrist and elbow joints are greased hinges, allowing you to move the slide in and out smoothly.

The technique is to lightly caress the slide grip using your thumb and first two fingers only. Not too lightly or you will lose your grip and the slide will fly off the end of the instrument like an out-of-control ballistic missile. It's like holding a small bird. Hold the slide too tightly and you'll kill it. Hold it too loosely and it will fly away.

Anyway, enough about trombone technique. How did I die? What killed me and how did I return from the dead?

Well, while playing my trombone I started to feel a tiny lump on the pad of my index finger. At first this lump wasn't anything to worry about but as time passed I noticed a white head appear in the middle of the lump. After about two weeks this lump with a white centre started to hurt. Not an 'I've-got-a-splinter' type hurt but more of a 'My finger throbs' type hurt.

I ignored this. The lump wasn't, after all, life-threatening or so painful that it rendered my finger unusable. It was just a bloody annoying irritation at the end of my finger.

However, after a few more weeks the white spot seemed to turn inwards, towards my finger nail, and the pain became more noticeable. More intense. To the extent that it was painful to the touch... And my finger started to throb

Although the pain was still tolerable, playing my trombone was becoming stressful. I found it difficult to concentrate on the music while my finger throbbed and the white spotted lump complained about me holding my slide grip. There was nothing for it but to report sick to see if the doc had any ideas to relieve the irritation.

I didn't realise, at the time, that my rogue gene was setting me up for a big fall... Literally!

The doc, a Captain, inspected my finger using a magnifying glass.

"We'll have that out, shall we?" he announced. Calling his assistant into the surgery he prepared an injection of local anaesthetic and bid me sit on a stool next to a table. With my arm resting on the table and my finger outstretched the doc injected the anaesthetic between my index finger and the one next to it.

"We'll just give that a couple of minutes to kick in," the doc says and turned round to prepare the tray of implements he needed to perform the minor surgery.

My finger started to really throb! In fact, my whole hand felt like it had been trapped in a vice.

Having prepared his tools-of-the-trade, the doc started his surgical procedure by slicing the skin on my finger pad either side of the lump.

"Soon be there," he said, and asks the assistant to stem the flow of blood. With a look of disbelief on his face the assistant exclaimed "Whoa! Look at that!"

I looked down at my finger to see a fat chipolata sausage poking out of the palm of my hand where my finger should have been. As I watched my forearm visibly swelling before my eyes an intense pain in my chest prevented me from taking a breath. Then... Nothing... Nothing but a darkness I had never before experienced. I couldn't feel my body but I could move my eyes to look round at my surroundings. Nothing but darkness... Pitch black. No! Blacker than pitch black. A darkness so black that it was impossible to see any light whatsoever, anywhere.

I was completely alone in the darkness. No sound, no light, just darkness. I wasn't scared, I was more intrigued. I tried to lift my left arm up to look at it but it wasn't there. It just didn't exist. Neither did my right arm exist or my legs or even my whole body! Just my eyes. That's what the darkness felt like. Nothing except my eyes...

I began to enjoy this darkness. Best sleep ever. No sound. No throbbing finger. Nothing. Then I thought to myself that I would miss music. I don't know why music, it was just a random thought that came to me in the darkness.

I became vaguely aware of being kissed. Was I back at home? Then I heard a distant voice. It was doc's voice. He was telling his assistant to, "Put something on that to stop it bleeding."

The darkness morphed into a sort of light grey steamed up bathroom window colour. And my ribcage hurt like hell. Like it had just been trampled on by everyone in the Battalion. My vision slowly improved and the cloudiness sharpened to full colour. I saw the doc on his knees next to me with his stethoscope pressed closely to my chest. The assistant was wrapping my throbbing finger with lint and squeezing it in the palm of his hand. I then realised that I was flat on my back on the surgery floor. My hands and feet tingled as if they were connected to a 9v battery and any attempt to move intensified the ache in my ribcage.

"Ah, you're back with us," the doc declared.

Although I was still extremely woozy I vaguely recollect being rolled onto a stretcher and evacuated to hospital in a speeding ambulance with the doc at my side. I kept trying to go back to sleep but the doc insisted that I stay awake. In a trans-like state, eyes half open and my brain half way from awareness, I heard the distant sound of the ambulance siren ordering everyone out of the way while I was rushed to the emergency department.

I was undressed by some unseen, unfamiliar person and put to bed. As I drifted unconscious once more I was vaguely aware that someone was attaching wires to my head and chest. I descended back into the envelope of darkness...

I felt disappointed when I opened my eyes the following day. I looked at my surroundings in puzzlement. Where was I? How did I get here? Why am I wired up to that machine staring at me from my bedside?

A gorgeous nurse with great legs appeared at my bedside with the words, "It's good to see you back with us Bandsman Pollard."

The nurse pressed a buzzer laying on the bedside next to me and she was immediately joined by several other gorgeous nurses with great legs. In some pain I was helped to sit up by the nurses, fussing over me with extra pillows and a smell of Dettol. One of the nurses brought me a cup of tea.

"You've missed breakfast," she said, "but lunch will be arriving soon. The doctor will see you in a moment. How do you feel?"

"Great," I reply. "Except for this pain in my ribs." The pain in my ribs was a pain that I recognised from the time I got a couple of broken ribs during my Junior Parachute Company days.

"That'll improve with time," the nurse stated. "You've got some broken ribs."

"How did I get those?" I asked with a puzzled look on my face.

"The doctor will explain all when he sees you."

"What time is it? How long have I been here?"

"I'm sure you have lots of questions, but the M.O. will explain all when he comes to see you."

I downed my tea and relaxed back to finish my snooze. After a short time the doc from Mons Barracks appeared at my bedside.

"You're looking a bit better than you did yesterday," he smiled. "More colour in your cheeks."

"What the hell happened?" I asked.

It turns out that immediately following my injection I went into anaphylactic shock, caused by a bad reaction to the local anaesthetic. While I was out of it, my eyes floating in the dark surroundings, some blood had been taken from my arm and transported to hospital with me. Tests had been made and it transpires that I am allergic to any Ester-based anaesthetics – Procaine, Cocaine, Tetracaine and the like. The tests also confirmed that Amide-based anaesthetics – Lignocaine, Lidocaine, Xylocaine, etc.

are safe for me, which is fortunate because today's modern dentists use this type of anaesthetic.

Nobody, myself included, knew that I was allergic to Ester-based anaesthetics until that fateful day. The doc had injected Novocaine and anaphylaxis had stopped my heart. Once in the hospital I slipped into a coma for a twenty four hour period.

It was a good job that the lump on my finger was being treated by someone who realised what had happened. The swelling of my finger and forearm, my collapse at the table, my lack of heartbeat and my inability to breath all pointed to anaphylaxis and the doc saved my life while I was flat out on the surgery floor.

And my broken ribs?

The doc had broken these while jumping on my chest to maintain a blood flow to my brain, and the kiss I thought was my wife's enticing lips was, in fact, doc's assistant blowing much needed oxygen into me.

Mind you, in many respects it was a good thing to find out that I am allergic to certain local anaesthetics at that particular time in my life, especially when I was being treated by someone who knew what he was doing. Any other time and I might not be writing these words...

Nonetheless, I bet my rogue gene got a bit panicky when he realised that his interference with my minor operation had gone too far.

It almost killed itself by killing me!

***

Has anybody out there ever had Piles? Haemorrhoids? A "bunch of grapes?"

If you get them once, you get them for life. Apparently most adults get piles at some time in their lives and in most cases the piles shrink back into your body after a few days. Nonetheless, they are a bloody nuisance. They're painful at the best of times, but even more so when you're having a dump. I usually dunk myself in a hot bath for a couple of hours and then give mine a hefty push back up into my arse. This relieves them and in most cases makes them disappear entirely, at least until the next time.

My very first brush with piles was when I was in Northern Ireland in the late 1960s. I don't know why my piles appeared at that precise time but they prevented me from having a crap for over a week. I had to go see my M.O., if only to get something to help me offload my week's worth of grub that felt like a huge full refuse sack inside my stomach.

I laid on my side with my knees up to my chin while the M.O. shoved his finger up my arse and wriggled it around. Yes, it was painful! The M.O. wrote out a chit and ordered a Land Rover to take me to the Royal Victoria Hospital in Belfast.

My arse was interrogated by a load of doctors and nurses. The poking and prodding and squeezing was relentless. Every day for almost a week. One morning a doctor brought a load of students to my bed and asked if it was okay for them to look at my Haemorrhoids. Seeing these things was part of the students' course lessons.

"Of course," I sanctioned.

The students circling my bed approached more closely to get a better look at my arse and one of them decided to take the initiative by parting my cheeks. He stuck his finger into my rectum and just as he bends down for a better view I say to the doctor, "I'm getting used to it. In fact, I'm beginning to enjoy it," with a smile, implying that my embarrassment at having the cheeks of my arse parted by a stranger's hands and having a finger thrust into my rectum was diminishing.

My joke had an unexpected effect. The student parting the cheeks of my arse at the precise moment I uttered this comment suddenly yanked his finger out and jumped back! Boy, did he look wide eyed and speechless. The other students' gazes oscillated from him to the attending doctor, eyebrows raised, waiting for some words of wisdom. The doctor ushered his students on to the next patient, leaving me wondering what I had done to upset them.

Now, what you must bear in mind is that being gay in the army at that time was illegal. It was frowned upon and any bloke who "came out" was immediately discharged from the army.

The consultant in charge of my case came round to my bed within a couple of hours of the students' lesson.

"I'm told that you've upset some of my students," looking at me menacingly over the top of his specs.

"Er, how?" I asked.

"Are you gay?"

"What! Absolutely not! Why do you ask that?" I protested, with more that a hint of indignation.

The consultant reminded me of my comment to the students and stood there, waiting for a response. I explained that I meant no offence, I was just being affable and co-operative.

"Oh, it's nothing," the consultant offered. "Just some idiot being a bit too sensitive." With that, he gave instructions about my treatment to his accompanying nurse and left.

I had to have an operation. A controlled anal stretch. A sphincter dilation.

That was more painful than the bloody piles. I'm not going to describe what's involved with this medical procedure, you'll just have to use your imagination. Suffice to say that it required a general anaesthetic.

I was in hospital for about two weeks after my operation. A couple of days after it I asked the ward sister if she had anything to help me have a shit, 'cos I hadn't had one for well over a week and it felt as if I had backed up to my epiglottis, like a blocked drain. She made me swallow two tablespoons of liquid paraffin... Awful stuff!

That did the trick, but the pain of having that first dump after my operation was so intense it drove me to claw and bang on the walls of the toilet cubicle while screaming in agony. A couple of nurses came rushing in to the toilet to investigate the noise I had made.

"Are you okay in there?" one asked.

"Of course I'm not bloody okay! I'm in agony, trying to have a shit!"

"Oh," the nurse replied, "It's only Bandsman Pollard. He'll be out in a minute," and they left me alone to suffer in solitude.

I eventually managed to finish my dump. With some relief I returned to my ward to rest my arse... And to repair my fingernails.

***

There were ten of us on the ward in the Royal Victoria Hospital, all soldiers from varying units with varying problems.

We all bonded well and had plenty of laughs, especially when we described our ailments.

One had had an ingrowing toenail. Another had been shot in the upper outer quadrant of his arse. We all had something hilarious to impart, except one guy who never took part in the late night discussions.

This guy was a bit of a party-pooper. No sense of humour and always complaining... No, moaning about his lanced boil. No stiff upper lip at all.

During one of our illegal late night soirees with the night nurses on the ward balcony, we hatched a plan to surprise this miserable excuse of a soldier. With a nurse's help we assembled the items required to hoax the guy. Our prank, however, produced a reaction that nobody could have predicted.

Here's what we needed:

- Some Gentian Violate - an antiseptic dye used to treat fungal infections (donated by the nurse).
- A spray can of artificial skin - this is like a thin plastic layer, sprayed over burns to keep the burn clean and help the skin's regenerative process (donated by the nurse).
- Small parings from a bar of soap (donated by the toilet).
- A teaspoon (donated by the breakfast delivery).

Shortly after Matron's ward inspection we mustered on the balcony to prepare our ingredients.

The soap parings had been left in a cup of water overnight to dissolve into a gooey mush.

The Gentian Violate was slowly stirred into this. A tiny drop at first to turn the goo into a greenie purple, then a few more crystals partially stirred to give the goo a streaky, science fiction type appearance. A big blob of this goo was then carefully spooned onto one of the bloke's forearm, and then sprayed with the artificial skin to keep it in place.

After several sprays of artificial skin this infectious disease looked really convincing. It was covered by the guy's dressing gown and he was ultra careful not to disturb his blister throughout the morning. We all carried on with our get-together on the balcony.

At mid-morning teatime the hypochondriac was invited to join us on the balcony. We even got him a chair to sit on 'cos he said he needed one. He told us that if he stood for any length of time he would fall into unconsciousness. Now this isn't a good thing for a soldier, is it? We needed to stand to attention for all sorts of reasons and for all sorts of intervals. The guys on the ward didn't believe him and were all convinced that he was pulling a fast one to leave the army on medical grounds.

We sat and chatted about nothing in particular for a while then one of the chaps asked another what he was in for.

"I got shot in my arse," he told us, exposing the upper-outer quadrant of one of his cheeks to show where the bullet had been removed. We saw the hypochondriac turn a little whitish around his gills.

Another guy jumped in with, "I've had an ingrowing toenail," planting a leg on the knee of the hypochondriac chap to show us his hugely bandaged big toe. Hypo' turns a bit paler.

We all explained our ailments, embellishing them to much laughter and mickey-taking.

When it was my turn I told the guys, "I've had my piles cut out," baring my arse to show everyone my operation scar that couldn't normally be seen. This created a roar of laughter.

Then the inevitable question was asked of the now quite ashen-looking hypochondriac.

"What's wrong with you, then?"

"I nearly died."

A silence descended on us all.

"Oh? Why's that?" someone asked.

"I had to have a dangerous growth removed from my shoulder." We all knew that he'd only had to have a boil lanced...

"Really? Let's have a look."

"Okay, but be careful because it still hurts."

"Oh dear," a sympathetic mumble from us all.

The chap gingerly exposed his shoulder to reveal a small scar where his boil had been lanced.

"Wow! That looks bad!" someone pronounced.

"Yes. They tell me I lost nearly a pint of blood when it was taken out."

"Phew! Do you know that you've only got about a leg full of blood left?"

"That's why they kept me in, to increase my blood count," lips now losing their colour.

By this time we were all splitting our sides trying to hold in our laughter and the strain was beginning to pull the stitches in my arse.

The hypochondriac's curiosity got the better of him and he asked the one bloke that had not given an outline of his 'problem', "What's wrong with you, then?"

"I've got a seriously infectious disease."

As the "infected" guy carefully removed his dressing gown to expose his "infection" we could see the hypochondriac beginning to wish he had never joined this party. He certainly wished he had never asked that question.

The infected guy stated, "It's okay. It's only highly infectious when it's been damaged so it's safe to show it."

With that he invited us all to "Feel it."

One by one we gave it a tiny prod and watched as the colours shifted inside the blob. The colour of the hypo's face also shifted, far away from the healthy spectrum.

The forearm went round to everyone. When it came to the hypochondriac the bloke said, "It's okay. See what it feels like but be careful not to burst it."

Again, the hypo's curiosity got the better of him even though he was now quite white.

He slowly and carefully touched the blob and with growing confidence he gave the edge a gentle prod. The infected guy exaggerated that prod by twitching his arm and guess what? The blob burst... All over the hypo's finger!

With wide, horrified eyes staring at the goo running down his finger the hypo' screamed and headed towards the door of the ward shouting "Nurse! Nurse! Aaaah!"

He never made it to the door because he just keeled over and landed like a bag of washing on the floor. He'd fainted.

The nurse appeared in the corridor and quickly went over to him. By this time, all the guys on the balcony were in helpless fits of laughter, tears streaming down our cheeks.

The nurse asked "What have you lot been doing?" and the 'infected' chap waved his 'infected' arm at her. With a disapproving smile she went to fetch a bottle of smelling salts and then helped the hypo' back into bed.

He never stirred from his bed until he was discharged from hospital the following day.

I bet his rogue gene was a bundle of fun.

***

Generally, my health hasn't been too bad since I left the army.

I've had a few knocks and scrapes, together with the usual ailments that folks get and I once had to go get my gall bladder removed. I suppose the worst thing that I've had is skin cancer behind my left ear. Once this had been diagnosed I had to attend The Royal Marsden Hospital in London to have it removed.

At the Marsden I was told that it was probably due to the many hours I had spent in the sun during my army career. This comment brought back a memory of when I was forced to remove my shirt in sunny Bermuda. I also remembered the times when my arms and neck got toasted while practising band displays on the square.

It is too late to sue the army now, though. Too much water under the bridge and the statute of limitations would prevent any successful action. Something else to curse my grown-up rogue gene about.

I had a course of radio therapy at the Marsden hospital, in London. This had the effect of making the tumour even angrier than it was when it first appeared. It went from being benign to being aggressive, so I had to go under the knife. I've now got quite a noticeable crater behind my ear.

That's okay.

Added to this is the fact that the radio therapy has compromised my immune system.

That's also okay 'cos at my age just being alive is a bonus.

Having said that, according to the internet the average age that men live to is eighty-three, so I've still got a few more years for my grown-up rogue gene to disrupt things.

CHAPTER THIRTY SIX

Bill's Coincidences

I thought I would leave all three of you with something to ponder over. Three is the sum total of people that I estimate have bought any of my books...

I couldn't determine where to put this final chapter. It's got nothing to do with holidays but I suppose it is loosely related to one of the other headings discussing communication or employment. It could have been stuffed into one of those sections, but it just didn't sit right in any of them so I've decided that it deserves a place all of its own in "That's Life." I thought it a fitting place for this chapter considering its obscure subject, and I thought it an appropriate place at the end of this final book about my life's ups-and-downs.

Suppose you unexpectedly meet a school friend in the high street, a friend you have not seen since you left school hundreds of years ago. Is that a coincidence? Was there any particular reason you both simultaneously decided to go to the high street on that precise day?

While you stroll head down in front of a bus as you swipe your index finger across the screen of your mobile phone, is it a coincidence that the bus that is going to squash you into the tarmac should be arriving at the same spot as you at that precise time?

Or maybe as you while away the time in the bath daydreaming about what a great time you could be having on some beach with somebody – your wife, your mate, your mate's wife – there is a knock on the door from one of the mates you've just been daydreaming about, arriving to invite you to take a joint holiday with them. Is that a coincidence?

If there is one thing that I'm sure about it is that the world is a small place. It was a small place even before the invention of telephones or the discovery of computers or appearance of the internet.

During my travels I've heard about, and even seen, coincidences that cannot in life's rich patterns just have "happened." Some coincidences must have been engineered by a higher being because I don't really believe that they exist in the natural course of events.

This thought is a bit deep, isn't it? But have you ever asked yourselves why you coincidentally meet a friend or relative while you are out just doing a bit of shopping? Did anything out there in the invisible dark matter decide it was time for you both to have an impromptu coffee by pushing you together in a crowded city centre? Who knows?

Was it a coincidence that my wife of fifty-two years just happened to be sat behind me in The Castle dance hall at Richmond when my mates persuaded me to go there, and then "dared" me to get up and have a dance with a complete stranger? Anyone! Who knows? Of all the women in that dance hall I chose the one who would still be with me fifty-two years after we got married... Even after I had courted her for two years before our wedding. Would any of the other women in that dance hall have stayed with me all that time? Who knows? Was it a coincidence that we were both in exactly the same room, sat at those precise tables at exactly the same moment? Who knows? Did that mysterious unseen being push us together on that random evening, when I could just as easily have remained back in my billet watching TV or studying my music? Who knows?

So what is a coincidence? Well, my Collins English Dictionary describes coincidence as *'a chance occurrence of events, remarkable either for being simultaneous or for apparently being connected.'* My Collins Thesaurus describes it as *'accident, chance, eventuality, fluke, fortuity, happy accident, luck, stroke of luck.'*

Was it a chance occurrence or an accident or a fluke or a stroke of luck that my wife and I met? Who can say?

But I can recall a few incidents that would question whether luck or accident or chance engineered coincidences that absolutely nobody can possibly explain.

***

Here's a coincidence for you...

Many years after I left the army I got a job as an Estate Manager for a housing estate on the outskirts of London. A big estate with many apartments and detached houses. I discussed this ill-fated job earlier.

Out of the blue a woman approached me during one of my daily rounds of the estate, and she said, "I've seen your piles!"

With a perplexed look, I asked, "What..? Why? How?"

"I was a nurse when you were in the Royal Victoria Hospital... And your piles weren't the only thing that amazed me!"

I think I might have blushed.

***

You might be thinking, "Well that wasn't much of a coincidence, was it? That type of thing happens all the time." Okay, here's a coincidence that will blow your mind...

During WWII my dad had postings to Libya, Egypt, Iran and Syria. Towards the end of the war, in one of those far away places, his unit apparently came across an abandoned Polish prisoner-of-war camp. The camp had been abandoned because the German army had retreated, had locked the gates and had left the prisoners to fend for themselves.

Dad related a story to me about the time he approached the locked gates of that camp and, after opening the gates, was confronted by a collection of bony starving men who didn't know if they were going to be saved or be shot. One of the prisoners staggered into dad's arms and he (the prisoner) was carefully laid onto a stretcher to be taken away by a field ambulance.

That "chance" exchange could not have taken any more than fifteen seconds but during that brief period something happened that would never explain why those two men were in that place at exactly that moment in time. Coincidence had pushed them together. Was it an accident? Was it a fluke?

Many years after the war had ended, when I lived in Sheffield, Dad went down to the city centre to get his watch repaired. Inside the watch repair shop the establishment's owner froze when dad entered.

With eyes wide open in amazement the shop owner declared to dad, "I know you!"

"No, I don't think so. I've never been to this shop."

"I recognise your face."

"Oh? Where do you reckon you've seen me, then?"

After a short pause for the guy to trawl his facial memory bank he dropped a bombshell that ignited dad's memory of a moment in time when the two men met for a brief period of only fifteen seconds.

"You were the soldier that opened the prison gates," the guy said, with tears in his eyes.

Dad took a few seconds to absorb what he had just been told. About the same amount of time that had passed at that first encounter.

In tears the two men embraced in a moment of recognition.

Dad's watch couldn't be repaired but the watchmaker always made sure that dad had a decent time piece to remind him to make regular visits to the shop, to drink tea and reminisce about their lives.

The two men remained devoted friends. A friendship that would last until they both died.

I think this shows that not only is it a small world... A very small world, but that rogue genes are not always as bad as the picture they paint!

Was it chance that made my dad go into that specific shop to get his watch repaired? There were, after all, many other watch repair shops in the city, some closer to the bus terminus than this one. Was it a fluke? Was it an accident or fortuitous?

Why did that watch repairer decide to live in Sheffield, of all places, after the war? Who knows?

Coincidence, or something beyond our comprehension, had pushed those two men together again. They were connected.
Connected by a war that both men had wanted to forget, but were brought together once more by a broken watch and a chance meeting.

***

Are you still convinced that coincidences are pure flukes in time and space?

Well, if you think that the previous coincidence was curious, what about related multiple coincidences experienced by me at entirely different times in entirely different places?

During my stint in the army I've been to many wonderful places. Places where you would never expect a coincidence to happen.

Believe it, or not, almost everywhere I've been posted around the world the same bloke has always been there before me. The incredible thing about these multiple coincidences is that the bloke in question, let's call him 'G', is my doppelganger! It's true.

I've never, ever, met this guy because he was always in a town, or a bar, or a restaurant before I arrived, whatever country I happened to be in and whatever town, or bar, or restaurant I happened to visit. This guy had been there sometimes mere weeks before I arrived.

I got to know about my doppelganger when I first joined the army. As a boy soldier I was based in Malta Barracks, in Aldershot.

Almost immediately I joined the band an instructor asked me, "Do you know G?"

"No sir, never met him."

From that time on I have been asked that question time and time again!

When I was at Kneller Hall (KH), in Twickenham, a Student Bandmaster asked me the very same question. There was absolutely no connection between my Aldershot instructor and the KH Student, but I didn't think anything of the enquiry at that time.

From KH I was posted to my parent band back in Aldershot. I was in the stores drawing out my Battalion kit and the storeman, a Sergeant, asked me the same question. This time my curiosity got the better of me.

"Why?" I responded when asked if I knew G.

"You look exactly like him. You would think he was your twin..."

Now this comment stuck with me throughout the whole of my army career.

I happened to go into the NAAFI while I was at the Parachute Regiment's Depot as an instructor, and the woman behind the counter said the very same thing.

"You could be his brother..."

I ascertained that G had been to that very same NAAFI just three or four weeks earlier.

What about this one, then?

I was in Tehran, of all places, with the band. In the Casbah there, while I was doing a bit of tourist shopping, a Danish soldier walked up to me and asked, "Do you know G? You really look like him!"

I asked how he knew G.

"He was in our camp cookhouse about a month ago... "

What the hell was G doing in a Danish army camp cookhouse? And who the hell was G anyway?

And another thing...

During one summer the band was leading a carnival at Basingstoke. A complete stranger, a woman, came up to me at the finish line and told me how she had followed me all the way round the carnival route just to ask how G was getting on. She had met him about a month ago and they went out for a drink.

I've had total strangers asking me this question in France, Bermuda, Northern Ireland, in fact just about everywhere my army unit had sent me. Who was this guy, and what did he do for a living? Why was he in those places?

If he was in the army what unit was he in? I never found that out despite a few discrete enquiries with my Company Office. They were not permitted to tell me. You have to admit, however, that that series of coincidences could not just have happened by chance or by accident. There were too many unconnected people, times and places for those coincidences to be fluky. And this guy had always, and I mean always, been there about a month before me so I never had the opportunity to catch up with him.

Curious, or what...?

What were the reasons for all the coincidences that I've just related to you? Why did they happen? Who knows? I don't. I've never found out but it sure is a small world, isn't it?

Bill's Epilogue

It is now May 2022.

I am seventy-two years old. Yep! Seventy-two years old on the thirteenth of May, 2022. Where the hell has all the time gone? What have I done with my life? Well, I suppose you could say that I've had the benefit of living through several lives and I've also accurately supported the mantra of that old adage, "I've got ten t-shirts." I mean that, literally.

- I've got some fond memories of my school life, not least the excitement of discovering myself and discovering just how randy schooling could be.
- I've had a life of being ambushed by a variety of women all wanting a bit of extra curricular activity. Ah, memories.
- For better or for worse I've had a family life, raising two children to adulthood, teaching them the difference between right and wrong and endeavouring to support them when their rogue gene interfered with their life's path. Like many parents, I've not always been successful with all that!
- I've had a life in the army. I've thrown myself out of aircraft flying at ridiculous heights and I've been to many foreign parts, met many foreign people and had many adventures. I've also been a respected army instructor.
- I've had a life of music. As an ace trombone player I've performed in The Royal Festival Hall, St Martins-In-The-Field, the Curium theatre in Cyprus and other prestigious venues, and I've been a respected music teacher. Since retiring I've established and conducted my town's own concert band and I've become a published music composer and arranger.
- I've had a life of university and further education and everything that that offers and I've become an educated idiot, with letters after my name.
- I've had a life of employment. I've been kicked, abused and knocked about but I've always picked myself up and carried on.
- I've had a life of self-employment. I've been a lecturer and a Health & Safety Consultant.
- I've had articles printed in notable professional publications and I am a published author.

- Finally, I've lived a life treading on eggshells, constantly wondering when, why and how my grown-up rogue gene will upset my applecart of quests.

I've got lots more t-shirts of events in my life...

I was in Bermuda when the Governor of Bermuda got shot in 1973. That wasn't me, by the way. I was posted to Northern Ireland during the troubles in the 1960s and 1970s. I have commemorated the D-Day Landings in France with my army band. I watched the Berlin Wall being demolished when East and West Germany was re-unified. I saw in the year 2000, a time when many people thought doomsday would descend upon the human race, and I have been invited to Nasa's Mission Control Centre in Houston, Texas, to witness an astronaut being transferred from the International Space Station to be shuttled back to earth.

I'm not going to bore you with these, but who else do you know has done this much... And loved every minute of it?

***

So, what messages from my memoirs have I tried to impart during observation of my life's accomplishments and catastrophes? Well, there are a few...

The first is, "Never stop trying."

Let me remind you of that old adage, "If, at first, you don't succeed, try and try again."

There is a lot of sense in this mantra. There will be times when you want to give up on your labours. Don't! You may consider taking an easier path, trying something different. Don't! Once you have a vision see it through. Stick to it.

If you have read my first book you will know that I once had a vision... A vision of being a military Bandmaster. My vision, however, was severely shattered when two people threw massively curved balls at me that ended my career.

I could have tried harder to keep that vision. There were other people out there that would have helped me, if only I had asked. I could have gone to a higher authority for help but I didn't. I took the easy path by resigning from the army. I curtailed a twelve year career by giving in to the pressure created by the actions of two men. What a waste of time that twelve years was.

Never stop trying...

My second message is, "Always look for the amusing characteristics of life. The humour of the situation."

Regardless of whatever obstructs your life's path there will always be something to smile about. My grown-up rogue gene has devoted its own life to complicating mine. It has grown up with me and it has interfered with many aspects of my life's development, but with each intrusion there has always been something to smile about.

So the moral here is, no matter how much you may be knocked down by circumstances, or disappointed by results, or frustrated by some unknown influence just smile... Regardless of what happens to you, or what your rogue gene manufactures for his entertainment.

Keep smiling...

My final message is directed to all those unfortunate individuals out there that have been endowed with a rogue gene.

Embrace it. Welcome it, even, because you are unable to evict it from your ball bag, or from under your arm pit, or from inside your ear, or from wherever else it happens to be reclining.

If you are one of those poor sods you will always have to duck and weave and dodge bullets and sidestep trouble. So get used to it!

I wish you all the very best of luck but you should, by now, recognise that luck just doesn't feature in anything in which your grown-up rogue gene has been involved.

***

Well, that's it. My life, laid out in front of you in two books... 'MY ROGUE GENE,' and 'MY GROWN-UP ROGUE GENE.'

I don't have any more anecdotes to give to you. I've emptied my brain of accounts about my travel through life's unending twists and turns and about the diverse ways in which I have managed to survive seventy two years of rogue gene nonsense.

I will, however, persevere with my endeavours to tame my grown-up rogue gene. I doubt that I will succeed but I remain hopeful that one day, perhaps, it will settle down to a life of retirement.

I sincerely hope that I have stirred some of your own old, forgotten memories. Perhaps you can even relate to some of mine? Look back on your life and rejoice in the knowledge that you are a unique and amazing person.

In the meantime I'll continue to look over my shoulder, ready to dodge the times when my grown-up rogue gene decides to poke its head above the parapet and meddle, some more, with my life...

Phew! You've reached the end of the musings on my life's trials and tribulations. I hope you enjoyed them.

Now go and make yourself another cuppa...

The End

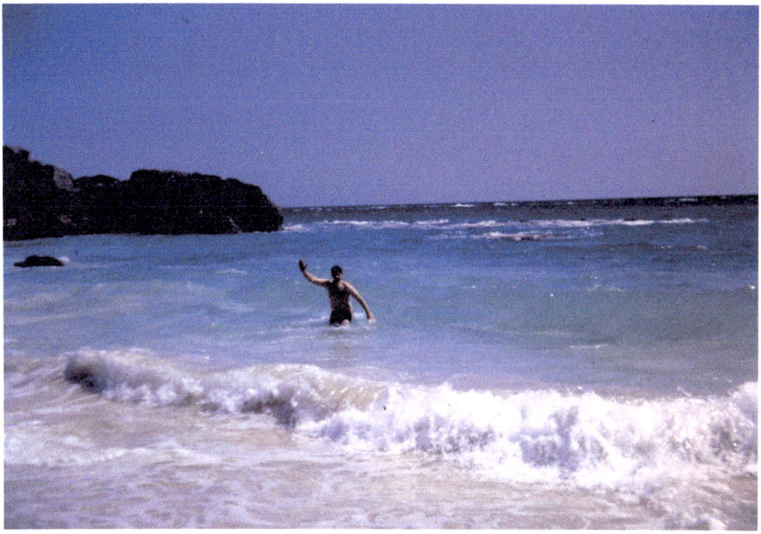